A
Woman's Guide
to Personal Holiness

Rhonda H. Kelley

Woman's Guide
to Personal Holiness

A Biblical Study for
Developing a Holy Lifestyle

Rhonda H. Kelley

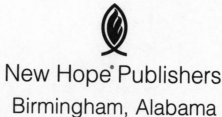

New Hope® Publishers

Birmingham, Alabama

New Hope Publishers
P.O. Box 12065
Birmingham, AL 35202–2065

Scripture quotations on pages 25, 43, and 47 are from the New Living Translation © 1996 by Tyndale Charitable Trust. All rights reserved.

All other Scripture quotations are from the NEW KING JAMES VERSION. © 1979, 1980, 1982, Thomas Nelson Inc. Publishers. All rights reserved. Used by permission.

Cover design by Steve Diggs and Friends.
Graphic Designer, Pam Moore.

ISBN:1-56309-432-0

A Woman's Guide to Personal Holiness

TABLE OF CONTENTS

PREFACE

In recent months, God has convicted me again and again of the sinfulness of my human nature. He has assured me that He is my only hope for godliness and that godliness should be a priority in my life. I have made a commitment to God, a commitment to myself, a commitment to my loved ones, and a commitment to you to be a godly woman. But I am reminded daily of my need to continually recommit myself to righteous living. Holiness will not just happen in my life. I must faithfully seek to be holy. A study of God's Word will teach me about His holiness and instruct me in daily holiness, but a personal commitment is essential to a life of holiness.

The Holy Spirit begins His work in the life of the believer when she is convicted of her sin and her need for salvation. He continues His work in the life of the believer convicting her of sinful behavior, guiding her in life decisions, empowering her in spiritual service, and providing for her personal needs. A study of Scripture and godly examples can promote righteousness. But a believer must depend on God alone and the power of His Spirit to develop and maintain a life of holiness.

While some Christians desire to be holy, others are less committed to the pursuit of holiness. Some Christian women even dread a life of holiness, thinking it means a life of rules and regulations or boredom. Nothing could be further from the truth. A believer's life need not be filled with negative discouragements, but positive encouragements. A woman of holiness learns to find great joy and satisfaction in her personal relationship with Jesus Christ. C.S. Lewis said, "How little people know who think that holiness is dull. When one meets the real thing... it is irresistible."

Join me in this biblical study of holiness, and make a daily commitment to a lifestyle of personal holiness!

—Rhonda Harrington Kelley

INTRODUCTION

For hundreds of years, Christians have spoken of holiness but many have not lived holy lives! Now it is time to return to the Scripture for instruction in holiness. It is time to stop talking and begin living holy lives in an unholy world.

This Bible study contains twelve lessons that examine the holiness of God and suggest guidelines for holy living. It is a topical study incorporating Old and New Testament passages about our Holy God and holy living. I've used a variety of sources in preparing the study to provide a comprehensive examination of this critical issue. In order to benefit from this study, several steps are essential.

1. **Commit to holiness**. First you must realize that God desires us to be holy. *"But as He who called you is holy, you also be holy in all your conduct"* (1 Pet. 1:15). Then you must make a personal commitment to holiness and renew that commitment daily. Without a sincere personal commitment, you will never become holy. You can also realize the joy that comes to the believer who obediently pursues holiness. So don't be afraid of becoming a holy person.

2. **Decide to study holiness**. While you may desire to study God's Word, you must discipline yourself to do it. So decide if you will complete this Bible study on your own or if you prefer to study with a small group. Then commit to complete the study you begin. A definite decision to learn about holiness is essential.

3. **Gather resources about holiness**. This Bible study book will be a helpful resource for your study of holiness, but you can benefit from additional resources, too. Select a Bible translation that you can use confidently or gather several translations to reference. (This Bible study uses the New King James Version unless otherwise noted.) You can refer to the numerous resources listed in the back of this book for additional study. Throughout the centuries, many Christians have written about holiness. You can learn from what God teaches others. You can also find additional resources on your own.

4. **Study and apply the Scripture**. Each lesson will focus on one specific aspect of holiness. However, each lesson will examine numerous Scriptures about holiness. Read the passages, study their meanings, and apply their truths in your own life. Each lesson encourages personal response and includes Scripture focus ("Holy Scripture for Holy Living") plus a section on practical application ("Personal Holiness"). The selected key Scripture is excellent for Bible memory. Each lesson should take thirty to forty-five minutes to complete. As you read each lesson, find each Scripture and answer every question, God will teach you about holiness. Try to complete one lesson in one week over a period of twelve weeks so God can make holiness a part of your everyday life.

5. **Discuss holiness**. This Bible study was designed for individual study, to be completed personally. However, discussion will make the study more meaningful. If you are participating in a small group study using this material, take advantage of the blessings that come through studying the Scripture with other believers. Anticipate God's work in your life and the life of your group. A group teaching guide is available for small group Bible study on page 80.

6. **Share your commitment to holiness**. While it is important for you to share what you learn about holiness with the Lord in prayer and with believers in small group study, it is also challenging to share your commitment to holiness as a witness to unbelievers. God wants to use your commitment to holy living to bring glory to Him and bring others to saving faith. So speak freely about your Holy God and His power for holy living.

7. **Continue to be holy**. When you have completed this study of holiness, remember that the process has just begun. You must persevere in your pursuit of holiness in order to live a holy life. God and others will hold you accountable for holiness. And God alone will reward you for righteousness!

8. **Enjoy the blessings of holiness**. Though the holy life is not always an easy life, it can be a joyous life. As you follow the example of Christ and obey His teachings, you will receive His blessings. There is no greater joy than the joy of the holy life. Godly Christian women can enjoy the blessings of holiness.

May God teach you about Himself and transform you into a godly woman! He can do that if you persevere in your Bible study and in your pursuit of holiness.

ISAIAH
6:3

*"Holy, holy, holy is the Lord of hosts;
the whole earth is full of His glory!"*

Christians are to be Christlike or little Christs. If that statement is true, then Christians must know what Christ is like. We must not only believe in Christ, we must also pattern our lives after Him. We must know who He is so we can become who He wants us to be. He is God in the flesh, sent to provide salvation for our sin. The Bible reveals that God is holy and we are to be holy like Him. So let's examine the Scripture carefully to better understand the holiness of God and the holy life He has called us to live.

WHAT DOES HOLY MEAN?

More than any other attribute, the Bible describes the holiness of God. All of His attributes flow out of His holiness. It is completely accurate and totally true to say, "God is holy!" What does *holy* tell us about God? In the *Holman Bible Dictionary*, John D.W. Watts suggests three biblical meanings of the word *holy*. Holy means "to be set apart," "to be perfect, transcendent, or spiritually pure," and "to evoke adoration and reverence." In this study we will use "being set apart for God" as the key meaning. Our God is certainly holy—set apart, perfect, to be adored!

In the Old Testament, the word *holy* (Hebrew word *quadosh*) appears 116 times and literally means "sacred, selected, pure." The very nature of God is pure, thus all of His attributes and actions are pure. He is the Holy One; there is no other like Him. His name is holy and His ways are holy. Because God is holy, He deserves our respect and worship and praise. The psalmist David proclaimed praises to the

Lord for His holiness. In Psalm 99:9, he concluded, "Exalt the Lord our God, and worship at His holy hill; for the Lord our God is holy." The Old Testament is filled with references about the holiness of God and His desire for people to be holy. While the human vocabulary is limited, the psalmist David and others tried to find words to describe the Holy God. We must study Scripture to better understand who God is. God is holy and holy is God.

In the New Testament, the word *holy* (Greek word *hagios*) literally means "set apart, sanctified, consecrated." While mentioned less often than in the Old Testament, the holiness of God is discussed in the Gospels, as well as several New Testament epistles. The work of the Holy Spirit is emphasized more in the New Testament than the holy nature of God. However, the writer of Hebrews affirmed the holiness of God clearly in Hebrews 7:26: "*For such a High Priest was fitting for us, who is holy, harmless, undefiled, separate from sinners, and has become higher than the heavens.*" The Bible—the Old Testament and New Testament—clearly states that God *is* holy. Holiness is not *what* God does, but *who* He is.

The contemporary world has a distorted view of the word *holy*, which actually comes from the Anglo-Saxon word *halig* meaning soundness and completeness. Today it frequently relates to health and wellness—physical wholeness. However, the dictionary does include a definition of *holy*: "exalted or worthy of complete devotion as one perfect in goodness and righteousness." God is thought to be holy by most people. He is respected and exalted even by those who do not have personal faith in Him. As the true Holy One, perfect in nature and action, He deserves deep love and devotion from everyone. As we better understand holiness, we can better express our devotion to the Holy One.

What does the word *holy* mean? You have reflected on the understanding of the word and Scripture regarding holiness, but take a few minutes before you continue your study to record your insights.

How do you think the world perceives the word *holy*? _____

_____

_____

Now write your own definition of the word *holy*. Holy means _____

_____

_____

Based on your own definition, do you believe God is holy? If you do, He should receive your devotion and praise.

HOLY—
SET APART

Reflect back on what the Scripture teaches about this term. Many biblical scholars say holy means "set apart."

What does it mean *to be set apart*? _____

_____

_____

Paul spoke in his writings about being set apart—being *in* the world but not *of* the world. Read John 15:19.

God clearly conveyed His holiness to the prophet in Isaiah 6:3: *"Holy, holy, holy is the Lord of Hosts; the whole earth is full of His glory!"* God is like no other. He is different, set apart. The repetition of the word *holy* emphasizes this attribute and elevates the nature of God beyond all others. He is literally "in a class of His own." He is set apart. As His children, God makes us holy by setting us apart for Himself. What joy!

Now read that entire passage of Isaiah 6:1–8 and describe the holiness of God in your own terms. _____

_____

_____

_____

_____

Picture God high and lifted up, seated on His throne—separated from all others by His holiness. The seraphim, or the six-winged fiery creatures who guarded God in His temple, proclaimed His holiness to one another. God's royal position and His righteous behavior separated Him then and now from all others.

Do you know someone whose godly life sets her apart from all others? Every believer should grow in grace and strive for sanctification, which is the purity we receive through the grace of God. As she does, her godly life becomes more obvious, more unique in this ungodly world. Throughout history, priests, nuns, and monks have been physically separated from the world so they could be spiritually holy. While God does not call all His children to life in a monastery, He does convict us to be different from the world because of our holiness.

HOLY— WITHOUT SIN

God is holy because He is set apart from all others. He is also without sin. It is humanly impossible to imagine that anyone could be without sin—blameless, perfect, spiritually pure. But the Scripture teaches that God who is holy is sinless.

What do you think of when you hear the word *sin*?

Circle any of the following phrases that would express your understanding of sin.

Sin is:

    a. falling short

    b. any act of rebellion

    c. selfish behavior

    d. getting caught doing the wrong thing

How do these phrases explain the meaning of sin? Ask yourself which is more fun, brings more happiness and joy—sin or righteousness? Reflect on the answers then return to the Scripture for true understanding. The Greek word for sin (*hamartia*) literally means "to miss the mark" or fall short of attaining God's standard. Romans 3:23 says, *"For all have sinned and fall short of the glory of God."* Only God is without sin; all others are sinful by nature.

God described His sinless character in His covenant with the psalmist David. If David obeyed His commandments, God promised to be faithful and merciful to him and his descendants. In Psalm 89:30–37, God assured David that He could be trusted because of His holiness.

Read that passage, then fill in the blanks below to describe the sinless character of God.

    verse 33—"My _____ I will not utterly take from him"

    verse 33—"Nor allow My _____ to fail"

    verse 34—"My _____ I will not break"

    verse 34—"Nor alter the _____ that has gone out of My lips"

    verse 35—"I have sworn by My _____ "

    verse 35—"I will not _____ to David"

God's holiness is reflected in His sinless character and His loving behavior toward us. He promised David, and He promises us that He will be kind and faithful. He will never break a covenant. He will be truthful and holy, and He will never lie. Though we are sinful by nature, untruthful and unholy, God can make us holy as we trust in Him and walk in Him. To be holy is to pattern your life after God's righteousness. Our God who is without sin is always holy. You can count on that.

Because God the Holy One is set apart and without sin, He should evoke awe from all believers. We should be filled not only with joy and praise but also with total respect and amazement. He is a mighty Creator and merciful Redeemer.

Ayers Rock in Australia inspires awe. It is one gigantic block of red sandstone in the middle of a vast and empty desert. Its beauty is magnificent. When I visited there, I was drawn to its grandeur. In the same way, our eyes should focus on God's creation and His character with reverence and awe. God deserves our sublime adoration because of His perfect holiness as well as His creative power.

Moses asked the Lord to reveal His holiness in a personal way, and God did. When he saw the glory of God, Moses was filled with awe. **Read this account in Exodus 33:12–23.**

In two distinct ways, Moses asked God to reveal Himself: *"Show me now Your way"* (v. 13) and *"Please, show me Your glory"* (v. 18). Desperate for help in leading the Israelites to the Promised Land, Moses cried out to know God's character and His will.

How did God respond to Moses's plea? Read Exodus 33:17 and describe God's response. _____

_____

_____

_____

_____

God honored the obedience and faithfulness of Moses by revealing His holiness and promising His presence.

Has God ever revealed Himself to you? Remember that time and record it here. _____

_____

_____

_____

_____

How did you respond to the Holy One? _____

_____

_____

_____

_____

Believers should always respond with the awe, devotion, and obedience that our holy God deserves. As we cry out to the Lord in deep love and adoration, He faithfully reveals His perfect holiness.

God has revealed Himself to me in many ways through His character and His creation. His pure, sinless, blameless nature sets Him apart from all others. And His beautiful creation reflects His power.

My husband and I recently traveled to Africa and visited Victoria Falls in Zimbabwe. Far in the distance, we could see the mist from the massive falls. Then we explored the one-and-a-half mile long waterfall discovered in the mid-nineteenth century by missionary David Livingstone. At each stop the view became more spectacular—a curtain of falling water, the winding gorge below, rainbows overhead, the thunderous roar of the water. As we rounded the last bend, we were amazed to see two complete rainbows. The sights and sounds reminded us of the power of our God. We were speechless. We were in awe as God revealed Himself to us.

As you reflect on times God has shown His glory and holiness to you, sing the chorus of praise, "Our God Is an Awesome God."

It is essential to remember that God is holy—He is the Holy One. The Bible teaches about the holiness of a perfect God who is separate and apart from others, who is totally without sin. It challenges us to respond to the holiness of God with reverence and devotion. Believers are to imitate the character and conduct of the Holy One. Holiness is to be embraced and not feared. It will bring a sense of wonder into your life. So embrace holiness with eager anticipation. In the next lesson, we will examine our own natures and learn to become a holy people.

Write and memorize the Scripture verse at the beginning of the chapter. _____

_____

_____

Are you consciously aware of the holiness of God? How does God reveal His holiness to you? _____

_____

Reflect on God who is set apart and without sin. Record below a prayer of praise to the Holy One, expressing your awe and reverence. _____

_____

_____

_____

_____

_____

1 PETER
1:15-16

> *"As He who called you is holy, you also be holy in all your conduct, because it is written, 'Be holy, for I am holy.'"*

A GODLY COMMAND

Christians are not surprised to learn of the holiness of God. There is confidence that He is set apart from all others, completely without sin. His holiness brings awe and reverence to the hearts of believers. However, believers are challenged when God in His Word calls us to be holy like Him. Holiness seems natural for God but totally impossible for people. God, who created us in His image (Gen. 1:27), desires us to be like Him—holy, righteous, godly.

Before we seek help in living a holy life, let's examine the biblical commands for personal holiness. As quickly as He confirms His own holiness, God challenges His children to be holy. It is natural for a father to desire only the best from his children. Thus, God intends for holiness to be a blessing and not a burden. God our heavenly Father not only desires our holiness but also empowers us to be holy.

In 1 Peter 1:13-21, the Lord, who breathed the words of Scripture, commands us to be holy.

Read this passage as an introduction to this lesson. Notice Peter's description of holy behavior and his assurance of God's power to give us hope and holiness.

First Peter 1:16 is the focal passage: *"It is written, be holy, for I am holy."* Peter learned this teaching personally from Jesus in the

Sermon on the Mount (Matt. 5:48). Jesus clearly stated that believers are to be holy in their natures, just as God is holy.

Look back at 1 Peter 1:13–21 to see how many times the word *holy* is used. Write that number here. _____

The word *holy* is written by the disciple Peter four times in this brief Scripture passage. Two times the word is used to describe God—*"He who called you is holy"* (v. 15) and *"I am holy"* (v. 16). Twice the writer uses the word *holy* as a challenge to godly living—"be holy in all your conduct" (v. 15) and "be holy" (v. 16). It is clear from Scripture that the believer should seek to be holy like God. In other words, we are to act like we belong to God. He set us apart for Himself.

Knowing that God loves *you* is a humbling thought. His love and mercy are personal. He offers salvation by faith to all, and His offer is extended to you and me. God's provision and power are also personal. He knows your needs and meets them in His time. In addition, God desires each one of His children to be holy. It is not enough for some to be holy. His heart's desire is for every child to be holy. His call to holiness is personal and persistent.

A holy God has called you to be holy (1 Pet. 1:15). You embraced His call to holiness at the time of your conversion and that call will continue throughout your lifetime. A *call* is an invitation from God to respond as He directs. God calls all to salvation and to holy living.

Read the following Scriptures and note a biblical teaching about God's call.

    2 Thessalonians 2:13–15 _____

    1 Corinthians 1:9 _____

    2 Timothy 1:9 _____

    Hebrews 9:15 _____

    1 Peter 1:15 _____

God has called you to salvation (2 Thess. 2:13-15) and to fellowship with Him (1 Cor. 1:9). He calls you to serve Him (2 Tim. 1:9) and to receive an eternal inheritance (Heb. 9:15). God's call is personal and specific; He calls all believers to be a holy people (1 Pet. 1:15).

Take a minute to reflect back on God's call in your own life. Record a brief testimony of God's call to salvation, service, and sanctification (holiness).

A CALL TO HOLINESS

My call to salvation: _____

_____

My call to service: _____

_____

My call to sanctification: _____

_____

A CONDUCT OF HOLINESS

Thank God for His call in your life—His personal invitation to salvation, service, and sanctification! I thank God for His call in my own life. At the young age of six and a half years, I accepted God's call to salvation. It was a personal call from God, not from my parents or a Christian friend. As a teenager, I accepted God's call to service. Though I didn't know exactly how I would serve, I knew God had a special ministry for me. My call to sanctification, which began at the time of my conversion, was renewed a few years ago when several friends failed in their personal lives. Now God calls me daily to holiness!

God graciously offers a call to holiness and the Scripture clearly gives a code of holiness. Specific behavior reflects a holy character. Christians are to conduct themselves in a different way than the world. We are to *be* holy and *live* holy.

The biblical term for the process of being made holy is *sanctification*. Sanctification begins at the time of conversion and continues throughout life as the believer seeks to be more Christlike. It is essential for you to thoroughly understand this important biblical concept. Let's consider three theological words that describe the experience of salvation.

Justification is the process of beginning a personal relationship with Christ through faith. Through justification, an individual is saved from the **penalty** of sin (Rom. 6:23). *Sanctification* is the process of being made holy like Him. In sanctification, the believer is saved from the **power** of sin (1 Cor. 10:13). *Glorification* is the process of becoming completely like Him when the believer is saved from the **presence** of sin (2 Cor. 3:18). Glorification comes to the believer only when you are with the Father in heaven for all eternity.

Do you understand these three important terms? If not, reread their explanations. Then try to explain them simply to a friend or write them here in your own words.

_____

_____

_____

_____

_____

The Old Testament talks about the sanctified life—a holy lifestyle. In the book of Leviticus many laws or guidelines are given by a holy God to promote holy living among His children.

Read Leviticus 19 and list below ten specific guidelines for holy conduct.

1. _____
2. _____
3. _____
4. _____
5. _____
6. _____
7. _____
8. _____
9. _____
10. _____

Like the Ten Commandments, these guidelines in Leviticus 19 direct our relationship with God and others. Believers should worship only God, keep the Sabbath, give offerings sacrificially, and obey His commandments. We should not take His name in vain nor harm His godly witness with our ungodly behavior.

Leviticus 19 instructs us to be holy in our relationships with others. We should honor our parents, care for the needy, be just and loving, and treat all people with respect. We should not steal from others nor lie. We should avoid hate and sexual immorality. We should honor God with our hearts and our lifestyles, not profane Him with our words or actions. A call to holiness leads to a conduct of holiness, but neither the call nor the conduct will develop without a personal commitment.

A COMMITMENT TO HOLINESS

Holiness begins with the invitation by God to be holy as He is holy. Then each believer must make a personal response. Commitment demands a choice of the heart and change in behavior. Thus when a believer makes a commitment to the Lord, a lifestyle change must take place—holiness. We are to strive to *"be perfect, just as your Father in heaven is perfect"* (Matt. 5:48).

Jesus Himself made a personal commitment to His Father. He determined to do God's will, not His own, even when it meant death. In the Garden of Gethsemane, Jesus made a profound commitment: *"Not as I will, but as You will"* (Matt. 26:39). The Son of God was not exempt from making a personal commitment. Believers are to commit to God's will—total surrender and true holiness.

As a Christian teenager growing up in a sinful city like New Orleans, I had to make a personal commitment to holiness. It wasn't enough for my parents to be godly or my friends to be Christlike. I had to make my own decision to be holy like my God. I remember that turning point in my own life when I decided to follow the holy lifestyle of Jesus, not the unholy lifestyles of those around me. That commitment made a difference in my conduct. I am grateful for my "boring testimony"—a life that was not tarnished by unrighteous behavior and deliberate rebellion.

In calling His disciples, Jesus demanded a commitment. He extended the personal invitation, but expected an individual response.

Turn in your Bible to Matthew 4:18–22, and read the call of Jesus to four disciples.

What was His call? _____

How did they respond? _____

How do you respond to the call of Jesus? _____
_____

Jesus clearly commanded that the fishermen follow Him and they responded obediently without hesitation. Jesus demanded a commitment from another person in Scripture—the adulterous woman. The Apostle John recorded the encounter of Jesus with the woman caught in adultery (John 8:2-12). When the scribes and the Pharisees demanded a verdict from Jesus, He spoke personally to the woman, offering forgiveness of her sin. Then He commanded her to commit to holy living—"go and sin no more" (John 8:11).

The adulterous woman received a call to holiness, which included a conduct of holiness as a result of a commitment to holiness. Have you made a similar commitment? God's holiness is without question. Our answer should be "yes" as we commit ourselves to holy living. God who is holy can make you holy too!

HOLY SCRIPTURE FOR HOLY LIVING

Write and memorize the Scripture verse at the beginning of the chapter. _____
_____
_____
_____
_____
_____
_____

Remember that you do not become holy on your own. God's working in and through you brings holiness. In the space below, record a commitment to holiness. Discuss your call to holy living and your plan for accomplishing that goal. Then sign the commitment at the bottom.

_____
_____
_____
_____
_____
_____
_____
_____
_____
_____
_____

Signature_____ Date_____

1 THESSALONIANS 4:7

"For God did not call us to uncleanness, but in holiness."

Young children often fantasize about what they want to be when they grow up—a teacher, a doctor, a nurse, a mommy. They have natural interests and desires. As we grow up, even as adults, we envision our lives as we hope they will be.

As a child, I always wanted to be a helper. I was my mommy's helper and pretended to be a nurse or a teacher helping other people. As a teenager, my personal aspirations became more specific. I knew I loved to talk and wanted to help others talk since communication was important to all human beings. So I began to explore the field of speech pathology. I completed my education preparing me for that profession then began working in the medical field in the area of communicative disorders. Speech pathology was my career, but ministry to people was my calling. Today God has focused that call more directly to minister to women.

God gives His children aspirations and professional pursuits, but He gives each child one clear goal for the future—a call to holiness. Holy living is not natural behavior for a child. We are born sinful in our very natures. If you doubt that statement, watch a young child who defies authority and seeks personal desires. Those selfish desires continue to control us into adulthood. Thus God calls believers to be different—to be holy. Again, let's turn to the Scripture for a biblical perspective on this call to holiness.

The apostle Paul ministered in a time of great ungodliness. There were no people more ungodly than the Thessalonians, whose sexual immorality was legendary. In that atmosphere of promiscuity, Paul wrote his letter to the Christians in Thessalonica challenging them to be different—to be holy in an unholy world. Paul reminded the early Christians that God's call to believers was for holiness not uncleanliness. The call of God to Christians today is the same. It is a higher call—a call to personal purity.

Read 1 Thessalonians 4:1–8. Underline key words or phrases that explain God's high call to holy living. What do you understand the Scripture to mean when Paul says each of the following commands?

"abound more and more" (v. 1) _____

_____

"walk in God" (v. 1) _____

_____

"please God" (v. 1) _____

_____

"possess your own vessel in sanctification" (v. 4)_____

_____

God extends to believers a high calling. Salvation offers more than a guarantee of eternal security. My husband says that salvation is more than a fire insurance policy and pew sores. It should bring about a change in lifestyle as well as eternal life. Paul said we are to *"abound more and more"* in righteousness after our conversion (1 Thess. 4:1). Believers are to *continue* becoming holy—living not in your own power but in the power of the Holy Spirit. With the help of God's Spirit, believers can uphold God's higher calling to sanctified living.

How are you doing in fulfilling your high calling to holiness? Using the exact phrases from Scripture, rate yourself on a scale from 1 to 10, with 1 being the lowest score and 10 being the highest. Evaluate your own response to God's high call to holiness.

"abound more and more" (v. 1) _____

_____

"walk in God" (v. 1) _____

_____

"please God" (v. 1) _____

_____

"possess your own vessel in sanctification" (v. 4)_____

_____

It is always sobering to realize how far you fall short of the glory of God. But don't spend too much time focusing on your failures. Recommit your life to the high calling of holy living.

Paul also spoke to the Christians in Philippi about holiness. He told them to keep pressing on in their spiritual growth. As believers forget the failures of the past and look ahead to a renewed walk with the Lord, holy lifestyles can be achieved. The goal is then accomplished and the prize is won: "the high call of God in Christ Jesus" (Phil. 3:12-14).

HOLINESS IS THE WILL OF GOD

Once a believer understands God's call to holiness, she often struggles with knowing and doing the will of God. While God's will does affect your vocation and daily choices, it also impacts your lifestyle. A godly lifestyle should set all Christians apart from the world. Paul reminded the Thessalonian Christians that God's will is for His children to be sanctified and holy.

Turn again to 1 Thessalonians 4 and reread verses 3 through 6. What is God's will for your life? _____

_____

State that in the following sentence by filling your own name in the blank.

"For this is the will of God, _____ *'s sanctification"*
(1 Thess. 4:3).

Generally speaking, God's will for all His children is to be holy. Specifically, holiness is lived out in different ways in individual lives. In another New Testament epistle, the apostle Paul gives specific instructions for Christians to do God's will.

Read the familiar passage in Romans 12:1–2 and paraphrase that passage below in your own words.

_____

_____

_____

_____

_____

Paul understood God's perfect will to be good, holy, and acceptable—a lifestyle different from the world. He passionately pleaded with the believers not to act like unbelievers, since God had done so much for them. In gratitude, God's children should live consecrated, righteous lives. Each believer is to make a personal sacrifice of self in order to be sanctified and serve the Savior.

While the world attempts to mold you into its sinful image, God wants to transform you into His holy image.

What are some of the temptations you face in the world? List a few ways the world has tried to conform you:

1. _____
2. _____
3. _____

Now ask God's forgiveness and recommit yourself to holiness which is the perfect will of God.

Sanctified living is the highest call of God and the perfect will of God. Our holy living also pleases God more than anything else we could say or do. It is tempting to think that our Christian service or our productive ministry is most pleasing to God. That is not true. A godly life is the greatest tribute to God.

My Christian parents express true joy when my life is committed to the Lord, and I am serving Him. My husband's parents are proud of their son, Chuck Kelley, and son-in-law, Paige Patterson, who are influential Christian leaders. Christian parents often pray diligently that their children will be involved in Christian ministry, but they must pray that their children will stay close to the Lord and rejoice when they live for Him faithfully. The joy of parents over the godly lives of their children is only a hint of God's pleasure when His children live holy lives.

Read the following Scriptures and identify what behavior pleases God.

Philippians 4:8 _____
Colossians 3:20 _____
Hebrews 13:21 _____

Paul received gifts from his Christian friends in Philippi—their generosity was *"a sweet-smelling aroma, well pleasing to God"* (Phil. 4:18). In another letter, Paul acknowledged that obedience to God's plan for relationships is *"well pleasing to the Lord"* (Col. 3:20). In a later New Testament letter, the writer of Hebrews said, *"Doing the will of God is well pleasing in His sight"* (Heb. 13:21).

What pleases you? While some material things or personal experiences may make you happy, true pleasure comes through expressions of love by other people. God is pleased when His children love Him and live for Him. A holy life pleases Him the most. A holy life demonstrates itself through unselfish generosity and faithful obedience. While good works are not the basis for a relationship with God, good works should flow from a relationship with God. Christians should respond to God's call to holiness because it is His highest calling, His divine will, and His deepest pleasure.

HOLY SCRIPTURE FOR HOLY LIVING

Write and memorize the Scripture verse at the beginning of the chapter. _____
_____
_____
_____ .

PERSONAL HOLINESS

What have you done recently that you believe truly pleased the Lord? Write that achievement below and explain why you believe God was pleased. _____
_____
_____
_____
_____
_____
_____
_____
_____
_____
_____
_____

Make a renewed commitment to please God through your holy living.
_____
_____
_____
_____
_____
_____

**LUKE
1:6**

[Elizabeth was] "righteous before God, walking in all the commandments and ordinances of the Lord blameless."

Throughout time, people have looked to other people for inspiration and encouragement. Our human nature is to place individuals who have excelled or succeeded in life on a pedestal, in a position of honor; they become role models to respect and imitate. Though personal rights and individuality are promoted, we naturally look to others as real life examples. Young or old, we have heroes.

A ten-year-old "boy wonder" named Gregory Smith recently gave his high school commencement address and challenged the graduates to imitate his heroes. His goal in life he said was to get three Ph.D.s so he could help change the world and eliminate violence. He passionately called his much older classmates to promote peace and love their enemies. He encouraged them to model their lives after his heroes: Martin Luther King, Mahatma Gandhi, and Jesus Christ. Though many people may marvel at this whiz kid, he desires to emulate those he sees as truly great. This hero has heroes.

Who is your hero? Who are some people you look up to because of their character and contributions? Christians need holy heroes who model the holiness of God. The Bible is filled with stories about holy heroes. History includes the accounts of holy heroes. Even today Christians can look up to modern holy heroes. These godly individuals are examples for us to learn from and role models for us to imitate.

Let's examine a few holy heroes in the Bible and others from more recent history. As you learn about them, think of women who have been role models for you in Christian living. Ask God to help you be a holy hero in an unholy world.

Though the Old and New Testaments are filled with examples of holy heroes, let's look in one of the Gospels at the lives of three godly women. Turn to the book of Luke and read about these heroines of holiness. Can you determine what characteristics and actions make them holy heroes? Each serves distinctly as a role model for a specific reason. If you imitate their holiness, you can be a holy hero too.

First, turn to Luke 1. Elizabeth, the wife of Zacharias and mother of John the Baptist, was an example for Mary the mother of Jesus and all Christian women because of her righteousness. She had a strong faith that was lived out in her daily life.

Read Luke 1:5–6 and determine why Elizabeth was found to be righteous before God. Record your ideas here. _____

_____

_____

_____

_____

_____

_____

_____

_____

_____

Luke describes Elizabeth as righteous before God because she walked *"in all the commandments and ordinances of the Lord blameless"* (Luke 1:6). Since she obeyed the Lord and lived a pure life, Elizabeth was a holy hero. She was determined to live by the law and follow all of its requirements. Because of her holiness, she influenced the mother of Jesus to accept the Lord's plan and give birth to the Savior of the world.

I know a contemporary heroine who desires to be found righteous before God. Her name is Iris Blue, and her testimony is powerful. She was drawn to the Lord as a prostitute and a convict because all she wanted was to be a lady. While in jail, this ungodly woman says she "knelt down a tramp and stood up a lady" as God saved her from her sin and made her holy like Him. What an example of God's mercy and grace. God used Iris as a dynamic witness in her ungodly world and now He uses her to challenge Christians everywhere to be holy. He can transform the unholy into holy and make each life a witness of heroic righteousness.

Luke's gospel includes the account of another holy hero. Anna, a widow of great age, served the Lord faithfully in the temple alongside Simeon, one who was "just and devout" (Luke 2:25). When Jesus entered the temple with His parents, Anna recognized Jesus as the promised Messiah. She was chosen to see the Redeemer because of her faithfulness and service. She was a holy hero who challenges us to *"live soberly, righteously, and godly in the present age, looking for the blessed hope and glorious appearing of our great God and Savior Jesus Christ"* (Titus 2:12–13).

Turn in your Bible to the story of Anna in Luke 2:36–38. After you read this Scripture passage, write a brief description of Anna.

_____
_____
_____
_____
_____
_____
_____
_____
_____

Luke describes Anna's words and actions. She spoke with confidence, proclaiming the birth of the Messiah, and she served God faithfully. God spoke through her and she spoke of Him. Anna *served God with fastings and prayers night and day"* (Luke 2:37). Her service was sacrificial and continual. She was respected and praised for her heroic service. She is a holy hero who deserves our recognition.

At the turn of the twentieth century, a missionary in China served sacrificially and continually. Called to proclaim Jesus Christ to the Chinese people, Lottie Moon served them unselfishly, giving all that she had to those people who had nothing. She worked with them faithfully for many years. At the age of seventy-two, she died of starvation so that her Chinese friends could have food. My own mother wrote this note in 1980 in my copy of *The New Lottie Moon Story*, encouraging me to model my life after the heroic service of Lottie Moon:

"My prayer is that you will emulate Christ Jesus who was glorified through Lottie Moon. May the power of the Holy Spirit lead you as you bless many lives!"

The examples of Anna in the New Testament and Lottie Moon, a missionary to China, challenge us to heroic service.

Another heroine is described by Luke. She also lived and ministered during the time of Jesus. She was an example of godliness in the time of the early church and continues to be a model of righteousness for Christian women today. Let's learn about her heroic commitment.

In Luke 10, you meet Mary of Bethany and her sister Martha. Read Luke 10:38–42. It is a familiar account that connects you immediately with one personality. Which of these sisters do you identify with and why? _____

_____

_____

_____

_____

_____

Growing up in a home with only one sibling—a sister—I often related personally to the biblical story of Mary and Martha. My younger sister, Mitzi, and I were just as different as Mary and Martha. I always identified with Martha—busy serving and helping in the kitchen while my sister was never in the kitchen; instead she focused on the guests in our home. What a reminder to me of proper priorities in life!

Jesus affirmed the commitment of Mary when He said, *"Mary has chosen that good part, which will not be taken away"* (Luke 10:42). In this encounter with Jesus, Mary of Bethany demonstrated her devotion to Him. In other Gospel accounts, Mary's commitment to the Lord is also recorded.

Read the following passages and describe Mary's heroic commitment.

John 11:1–44 _____

_____

_____

John 12:1–8 _____

_____

_____

Mary of Bethany has lived throughout history as an example of godly commitment. When the Lord visited her home, she gave Him her undivided attention (Luke 10:39). When her brother Lazarus died, her faith in the Lord did not waver. She expressed confidence in His miraculous power when she said, *"Lord, if you had been here, my brother would not have died"* (John 11:32). And Jesus demonstrated His power when He raised Lazarus from the dead.

22

In a later encounter, Mary's devotion prompted her to anoint the feet of Jesus with a costly oil. Her sacrificial act of commitment gave Jesus the opportunity to teach His disciples about His approaching death on the cross. The gospel of Matthew records the praise of Jesus for Mary's heroic commitment: " *'Assuredly, I say to you, wherever this gospel is preached in the whole world, what this woman has done will also be told as a memorial to her'* " (Matt. 26:13). Christian women today should strive to be committed to Jesus Christ like Mary—always sitting at His feet.

Though commitment is not a common quality in people today, devotion to the Lord has characterized some contemporary women. One committed woman of faith lived in Holland during World War II. Her name was Corrie ten Boom. *The Hiding Place* tells her story of a family's commitment to protecting Jews from the German Gestapo. After Corrie ten Boom was discovered by the Nazis, she spent almost one year in a concentration camp. During her time of persecution, she clung to her faith for survival. "Lord Jesus, protect me!" was the plea she recorded in her journal. Her commitment never faltered though she lost her parents and her sister, Betsie. During her imprisonment and for the rest of her life, Corrie ten Boom's extraordinary commitment and devotion to God resonated in her words of testimony. Her commitment was heroic when she was confronted to share the gospel with a German soldier who had tortured her. She wrote:

> *"Jesus Christ had died for this man; was I going to ask for more? Lord Jesus, I prayed, forgive me and help me to forgive him....And so I discovered that it is not on our forgiveness any more than our goodness that the world's healing hinges, but on His. When He tells us to love our enemies, He gives, along with the command, the love itself."*

Many women of the Bible provide examples of godliness for us today. If you haven't read lately about the lives of some holy heroines in the Bible, I encourage you to do so. My Bible study entitled *Life Lessons from Women in the Bible* could be a helpful guide to you as you search the Scripture for godly role models. You should also notice holy heroines living in your world. They can encourage you in your journey of holiness and motivate you to be an example of holiness to others.

HOLY SCRIPTURE FOR HOLY LIVING

Write and memorize the Scripture verse at the beginning of the chapter. _____

_____

_____

Whom do you look up to as a holy hero? Identify that individual and describe why in the space below. _____

_____

_____

_____

_____

_____

_____

_____

_____

_____

_____

Spend some time in prayer reflecting on the powerful influence you, as a woman living in holiness, can have. Consider your own level of righteousness, service, and commitment before God. Aspire with God to reach your full potential as a holy hero.

COLOSSIANS 3:12

"Since God chose you to be the holy people whom he loves, you must clothe yourselves with tenderhearted mercy, kindness, humility, gentleness, and patience."

How does a Christian develop holiness? What a challenging question! It is a question that Christians must ask and attempt to answer. Before we specifically identify holy habits, let's discuss the development of holiness in the lives of Christians. The best answer to the "how" question comes from a key word in the definition of the biblical term *sanctification*. According to the *Holman Bible Dictionary*, *sanctification* is "the process of being made holy resulting in a changed lifestyle for the believer." The key word is *process*. Developing holiness is the process of becoming like Christ. It is this ongoing process in the believer's life that results in a lifestyle of holiness.

The dictionary defines *process* as "something going on" or "a natural phenomenon marked by gradual changes that lead toward a particular result." Several things about a process are clear in these definitions. 1) A process is active and it takes time; 2) a process is gradual; and 3) a process results in change. Holy living is truly a process—gradual steps of faith resulting in a changed life.

In his letter to the Christians in Colossae, the Apostle Paul talked about the process of sanctification . He challenged believers to "put off the old man" and be renewed in the image of God (Col. 3:9–10). In the third chapter of this epistle, Paul used several words that denote the ongoing process in sanctification. He repeated his theme of developing holiness several times in this brief passage.

Read Colossians 3:1–14 and underline key words or phrases that describe the process of sanctification. Now list below several descriptors of this process. _____

_____

_____

_____

_____

_____

_____

_____

Paul identified at least three steps in the process of sanctification. If you are to develop holiness you must:

1. Put sin to death—die to your old sinful self.
2. Take off ungodliness—no longer live in sin.
3. Put on godliness—live now in righteousness.

From the point of a person's conversion until the time of her death, God is making His holiness complete in believers. Now let's carefully examine this process of holiness in Colossians 3.

PUT SIN TO DEATH

After Paul exhorted Christians to *"seek those things which are above"* and *"set your mind on things above"* (Col. 3:1-2), he told us how to do it. The first step is "put sin to death." Colossians 3:5 says, *"Therefore put to death your members which are on the earth."* The phrase translated "put to death" actually comes from the Greek word *nekron* which means to "reckon as dead." Paul was not actually calling Christians to commit suicide or kill themselves. Instead, he explained that the process of sanctification requires extinguishing evil desires and actions.

What are some of the sinful behaviors that Paul said the believer is to put to death? Reread Colossians 3:5. Then list some of the sins that should no longer be a part of the believer's life. _____

_____

_____

_____

_____

_____

Paul reminded the believer that immorality, impurity, passion, evil desire, greed, and idolatry are sinful behaviors which should no longer be a part of the believer's life. Remember, too, this list of carnal behaviors is not exhaustive. In other passages, Paul listed even more sinful behaviors. All sin is to be put to death after salvation. We are to die daily to sin.

Do you understand the practical application in this biblical teaching about the process of sanctification? To develop holiness, a believer must strive to eliminate all ungodliness—all sinful thoughts or deeds—through the power of the Holy Spirit. When sin is put to death, it no longer exists. Once this is done, holy habits can be developed.

TAKE OFF UNGODLINESS

Paul added another step to this process of sanctification. After you put sin to death in your life, you must keep on taking off ungodliness. In Colossians 3:8-9, Paul strongly reminded Christians to put off all these things. The process of sanctification continues after the believer extinguishes sinful behavior because sinfulness keeps returning. The believer must daily take off ungodliness. The phrase "put off" or "take off" is associated with the everyday task of dressing, when clothing articles are taken off and put on by the wearer.

Paul reminded Christians that the believer must personally take off ungodliness. Colossians 3:8 says that you must do it. It would be so much easier if someone else could do this hard work for us. But the believer herself is responsible for removing sinfulness from her life. Each of us will be held accountable by God for the sinfulness of our own lives.

What ungodly behaviors must the believer take off in order to be holy? Read Colossians 3:8–9. Then list below each act of ungodliness that Paul said to take off. Beside each ungodly behavior, list a personal example of that unholy behavior.

	Sin	**Example**
1.	_____	_____
2.	_____	_____
3.	_____	_____
4.	_____	_____
5.	_____	_____
6.	_____	_____

Now ask God to forgive you of your sin. Put off that ungodliness in your life.

PUT ON GODLINESS

Paul cited specific sins of the Christians in Colossae in this passage. Many of those same sins continue to be a problem for Christians today. We must keep on extinguishing or removing from our life these sins of the spirit and the body. Paul listed these sins of the body: sexual sin, uncleanliness, passion, lustful desire, greed, and idolatry. These sins of the flesh result from an ungodly spirit, but sin often begins in the heart with ungodly thoughts and feelings. Ask God to help you control your own unholy behaviors.

The final step discussed by Paul in this process of sanctification is putting on godliness. Holy habits cannot be worn until unholy habits are removed. The Scripture gives positive instruction in righteousness.

Read again Colossians 3:12–14 to identify a believer's spiritual wardrobe. Listed below are the eight virtues a believer is to wear in order to be holy. Describe what each one means to you.

1. tender mercies _____
2. kindness _____
3. humility _____
4. meekness _____
5. longsuffering _____
6. tolerance _____
7. forgiveness _____
8. love _____

Every believer is to put on "tender mercy." The Hebrew word *chesed* which is translated "mercy" literally means unfailing love. Do you wear tender mercy daily? "Kindness" has been defined as "steadfast love expressed in action." Do you express love consistently in your actions? "Humility" or total dependence on God and respect for others, not yourself, is to be worn by the believer. Does humility characterize your countenance? "Meekness" is best described as "strength under control." Is your strength always under the control of God?

The Greek word for "longsuffering" or patience actually means "bear up under." Are you able to bear up under the challenges of your life? The believer is to put on "tolerance" or endurance of people, things, and circumstances. Can you tolerate even the most difficult people and the most challenging circumstances? The "forgiveness" which is from God should be complete, everlasting, readily available. Do you forgive others freely and without conditions? Paul concludes this spiritual wardrobe with the most important garment—he says to put on *love*. True love, biblical love, is the finishing touch, which makes the believer's ensemble complete or perfect. Do you put on love every day?

How do you feel when you add a finishing touch to your ensemble? Maybe you put on the perfect pin, an attractive accessory, or some shiny new shoes. You feel great as your wardrobe comes together. A Christian should feel grateful as each garment of the spiritual wardrobe is put on.

(You can learn more about the spiritual wardrobe from the study of *A Woman's Guide to Spiritual Wellness,* the first book in this Bible study series.) Daily discipline is required to continue putting on godliness. Abiding in Christ enables you to put on and wear your spiritual wardrobe.

The psalmist gave instruction about developing holiness in Psalm 119:9–11. A believer is to keep her ways pure by obeying His Word, seeking His will, and abiding in His love. As the believer focuses on the positive traits to develop, she will not be discouraged by the negative behaviors to avoid. A life of holiness yields great joy. The Christian life is not a commitment to a boring life.

As you conclude this study, make a commitment to God to pursue this process of sanctification. You will need to renew this commitment regularly. Discipline yourself daily to develop holiness as you put sin to death, take off ungodliness, and put on godliness. You will discover that the development of holiness takes time. As Erwin W. Lutzer said, "There are no shortcuts to maturity. It takes time to be holy." But it is an investment of time that will bring forth great dividends in your personal life. Sing the words to this chorus as a closing response.

"Take Time to Be Holy"

Take time to be holy,
Speak oft with the Lord;
Abide in Him always,
And feed on His Word:
Make friends of God's children,
Help those who are weak;
Forgetting in nothing
His blessings to seek.

HOLY SCRIPTURE FOR HOLY LIVING

Write and memorize the Scripture verse at the beginning of the chapter._____

_____

_____

PERSONAL HOLINESS

List below those personal behaviors that God has convicted you to put to death, take off, and put on.

Put to Death _____

Take Off _____

Put On _____

Now pray that God will develop in you His holiness.

1 JOHN
2:15

"Do not love the world or the things in the world."

You don't have to look far to be reminded that we are living in an unholy world. Newspapers, magazines, television, and radio document the low level of human behavior today. In just a matter of days, the newspapers published the following headlines confirming an epidemic of unholiness.

"Security Guard Kills Neighbors and Self"
"Is It a Mad, Mad World?"
"Second Trial Opens in Murder of Gay Man"
"Some Fear Lack of Action Will Bring Hate Epidemic"
"Poverty Faces Most Newborns in the World"
"School Board Strengthens Discipline Code"
"New Law to Battle Product Piracy"

While the Bible challenges Christians to be in the world but not of the world (Rom. 12:1–2), holy rather than unholy, the reality is that the world bombards us with its unholiness. Sin is rampant and ungodliness is raging. A believer's greatest life work is resisting personal temptation and overcoming evil with good. But evil and wickedness are a natural part of human nature. They are intensifying in the world and confronting the Christian.

The editor of a tabloid newspaper was brainstorming with his writers about a sensational headline. For a moment, they were stumped. It seemed that there had been no scandal, gossip, or personal calamity to report. With confidence, the editor assured his staff that a shocking headline would come—it always did. Sadly, he spoke from years of experience when he said, "You can always count on human nature for a scandal."

Since sin entered the world, it has been unholy—filled with scandal. And the unholy world has influenced Christians who have difficulty resisting sinful temptation. While there is little need to study about unholiness because it is so evident, Christians should turn to the Bible for guidance. Scripture, like the newspapers, records the sinful living of pagans and rebellious behavior of believers. Instead of focusing on unholiness though, let's examine what the Bible teaches about temptation, testing, and triumph over sin.

Sin came into the world in the Garden of Eden. When Satan tempted Eve and Eve tempted Adam, the pattern was established (Gen. 3:1-19). No longer perfect and sinless, man and woman will inevitably face temptation and commit sin. Every person is tempted by someone or something. The world is filled with temptations which makes sin an ever-present enemy of the believer. With the introduction of the Internet, temptation to sin is even greater in the privacy of your own home.

What does the Bible teach about temptation?
Read 1 John 2:15–17. Then answer the following questions.

How does this Scripture describe temptation? _____
Who is the tempter? _____
What is the result of temptation? _____

The Woman's Study Bible defines *temptation* as "an enticement to sin that arises from human desires and passions." Temptation comes in a variety of shapes and forms—thoughts, feelings, and actions. The tempter is the devil who is cunning and deceitful (Matt. 4:3). He quickly identifies human weakness and personalizes temptation in order to ensure the person's fall. Temptation was first recorded in the Book of Genesis and persisted throughout Scripture. Satan was so bold to even tempt Jesus Christ, the Son of God (Matt. 4:1-11). But Jesus proved that the power of God can triumph over temptation. When sin entered the world through Eve, we were taught that Satan tempted, but Eve tasted.

The apostle John wrote and taught a lot about temptation. He warned the disciples and Christians in the early church about the temptations of the world and the flesh.

TEMPTATION

Underline the key words or phrases in the passages below where John warned about sin and worldliness.

John 15:19: *"If you were of the world, the world would love its own. Yet because you are not of the world, but I chose you out of the world, therefore the world hates you."*

John 16:33: *"In the world you will have tribulation, but be of good cheer, I have overcome the world."*

John 17:15: *"I do not pray that you should take them from out of the world, but that you should keep them from the evil one."*

1 John 2:15: *"Do not love the world or the things in the world. If anyone loves the world, the love of the Father is not in him."*

1 John 3:6: *"Whoever abides in Him does not sin. Whoever sins has neither seen Him nor known Him."*

TESTING

Christians are to resist the temptation of the world—to avoid sinful influences whenever possible and to depend on the power of God to overcome the evil one. But the world is unholy and the devil is at work. God gives His children protection against warfare.

Read Ephesians 6:10–17 out loud. Claim this Scripture as your own as you resist temptation.

This unholy world is filled with temptation and with testing. While temptation is the enticement to sin, testing involves obstacles that challenge the believer's personal relationship with the Lord. Testing begins at the time of conversion and continues until the believer is in the presence of God in heaven. Trials and tests of the faith can strengthen the believer (Jas. 1:2-4). Tests come in a variety of forms: tests of knowing Him, tests of living for Him, and tests of serving Him.

John wrote very personally about the test of knowing God in 1 John 2:3–11. Read this passage in several translations. Then paraphrase it briefly in the space below. _____

_____

_____

_____

_____

One way that the devil tests believers is to prompt them to question their own salvation. Doubt, worry, and fear may cloud the mind of an immature Christian. Believers must cling tightly to the truth that salvation is secure. Once a person trusts the Lord as Savior, salvation is sure. The evil one and this unholy world will cast doubt and point blame if a believer does not show by her life that she is Christ's follower. The apostle John confirmed the permanency of salvation and the evidence of salvation. *"Now by this we know that we know Him, if we keep His commandments"* (1 John 2:3).

Believers also experience the test of living for Him. It is so much easier to live life on your own terms and live like the world. But Christ calls Christians to a higher calling—holy living. Consistency in godly living will be tested. The devil will place obstacles to righteousness in the believer's path. He will challenge decisions and confuse thoughts in an attempt to seduce believers to his evil way. In 1 John 2, the apostle states clearly that the believer is to *"know Him"* (v. 3), *"love Him"* (v. 5), *"abide in Him"* (v. 6), and *"walk in Him"* (v. 6). You must live for the Lord and not just trust in Him as Savior.

Write your name in the blanks that follow and then read this personalized Scripture aloud as a prayer.

If_____ says she abides in Him then_____ ought to walk just as He walked (1 John 2:6).

Put this verse with your name on a card and place it where you will notice it often and be reminded of your commitment to holiness.

Tests of faith face the believer who is trying to serve the Lord. While serving the Lord ought to be a blessing for the believer, ministry can often become difficult and burdensome. The devil will not only test our call to Christian service, but he will also question our motives and diminish the results. Tests of service confront even the most devoted, active servant of the Lord.

First John 2:5-6 is a promise for believers who are being tested. As you abide in Him and walk in His ways, you will grow in knowledge of Him. You will faithfully live for Him and sacrificially serve Him. What a great promise to claim as we respond to the testing of our faith!

Though temptation and testing are inevitable in this unholy world, the believer must be reminded that God can triumph over the devil and his distractions. The believer must always be on the alert and consistently attest to faith in words and actions. The power of God is available to believers

TRIUMPH

34

who want to conquer sin. As the Scripture proclaims, *"Greater is He that is in you than he that is in the world."*

The Christians of the early church in Rome lived in an unholy world. They faced sinful temptation and spiritual testing. Paul wrote to encourage them to cling to their faith, remembering the high cost of sin. He used a familiar analogy from the slave market to help them understand the seriousness of their commitment to God. In Romans 6:15-23, Paul declared we are all slaves, either to sin or to God. When sin controls your life, you are a slave to unrighteousness. When God controls your life, you are a slave to righteousness. God can set you free from sin and give you the fruit of holiness. What a victory over death and sin!

Read the following Scriptures and note what they teach about triumph over temptation and testing.

     Romans 8:2   _____
     John 8:34–36   _____
     John 8:31–32   _____
     Romans 5:9   _____
     Galatians 5:13–14 _____
     Romans 6:23   _____

Christ Jesus is the One who sets a believer free from sin (Rom. 8:2). We no longer have to be slaves to sin (John 8:34-36). His truth can set us free (John 8:31-32). We are free from the judgment of God (Rom. 5:9) and are free to serve Him and others (Gal. 5:13-14). Through Christ we can triumph over sin and death (Rom. 6:23).

It is easy to feel oppressed in this unholy world, but there is *freedom* when you are a slave to God. It is natural to face temptation from the people and things of this world, but God can help you resist sin. It is common to question God and His work in the world, but He reassures you in these tests of faith. He can and will triumph over temptation and testing in your life.

How are you being tempted and tested? What entices you to sin? What challenges your faith? Circle the phrases below that describe your own sinful nature.

    1. **envious feelings**
    2. **sinful thoughts**
    3. **ungodly actions**
    4. **unkind words**
    5. **selfish passions**
    6. **other** _____

Has God helped you triumph over those ungodly thoughts and actions? Remember that He overwhelmingly conquers as you depend on Him to resist temptation.

As G. Campbell Morgan once said, "Holiness is not freedom from temptation, but power to overcome temptation." Make a personal commitment to resist temptation. Allow the Holy Spirit to make you a holy person in an unholy world. Experience the power of the Holy Spirit to overcome temptation and develop holiness.

Write and memorize the Scripture verse at the beginning of the chapter. _____
_____
_____

Select a statement below that you can commit to memorize and recall every time you face temptation in this unholy world.

"I will be holy in this unholy world."

"God desires me to be holy, for He is holy."

"I will be holy in all my conduct."

"I will resist those temptations that lead to unholiness."

"God can help me overcome even my greatest temptation."

"With God's help I will triumph over temptation."

Circle the statement that you selected. Now read it aloud prayerfully. God will bring it to your mind as you encounter temptation.

LUKE 9:23

"If anyone desires to come after Me, let him deny himself, and take up his cross daily, and follow Me."

By this time in our study you may be convicted about your lack of holiness and your tendency to sin. Don't be discouraged! Once God convicts you of your sinfulness, He begins to work in your heart and life to make you more like Him. Remember, *"If we confess our sins, He is faithful and just to forgive us our sins and cleanse us from all unrighteousness"* (1 John 1:9). God can help you develop holy habits and live a holy lifestyle.

Becoming holy like God is a process. It is not just a one-step, short-term process. It is an ongoing, daily process. The believer must make a daily commitment to live a godly life if she is to resist temptation and be holy. The commitment must be sincere, serious, and specific. You must mean it before you can do it!

Before we go any further in this study, you must answer this very direct question:

Have you made a genuine commitment to holy living? Write your honest answer here. _____

_____

_____

_____

_____

If you answered "yes" to the question on the previous page, add to that commitment a promise to renew your personal commitment to the Lord *daily*. If you do not recommit yourself daily to a life of holiness, the world will have a stronger influence on you. If you do not make it a wholehearted commitment, you will not develop holiness.

In his suspense novel entitled *Compelling Evidence*, Steve Martini said, "The trouble most people have with resisting temptation is that they never really want to discourage it completely." This seems so true in our world and the Christian community. Even believers want to walk the line, live on both terms, and dabble with sin. Do you want to discourage temptation in your life? Do you sincerely want to be holy? If not, God will continue to convict you and correct you. If so, you must practice daily, the dedicated disciplines of holiness. Let's examine each step toward holiness.

DAILY

Daily literally means every single day—without exception. What things do you do *daily*? Each of us performs important tasks daily. These are some things you do daily: breathe, brush your teeth, eat, dress, and bathe. You do them daily because they are necessary for your health and well-being. The Bible teaches that Christians must practice godliness daily if you desire to grow and thrive in your faith. Daily holiness is necessary for your spiritual health and vitality.

Look up a few Scriptures that instruct Christians on what to do and how to live daily. Beside each reference, record a life lesson to be practiced every day.

Psalm 61:8 _____

Psalm 72:15 _____

Psalm 88:9 _____

Isaiah 58:2 _____

Luke 9:23 _____

Acts 2:46–47 _____

Acts 17:11 _____

Hebrews 3:13 _____

Scripture teaches that believers must behave in a certain way daily. In the Old Testament, we are taught to uphold our vow or commitment to God daily (Ps. 61:8). We should praise the Lord and call upon Him daily (Ps. 72:15; 88:9). Prayer and praise are daily habits of the holy. We should seek Him and His will daily (Isa. 58:2). The New Testament teaches us to worship Him daily, remaining constantly in His presence (Mark 14:49). We should take up the cross every day, dying to self and following Him (Luke 9:23). Christians in the early church demonstrated that we should gather together daily for fellowship and worship (Acts 2:46–47). We should study the Scripture daily to know the truth (Acts 17:11). And we should encourage and minister to each other daily (Heb. 3:13; 10:11). The days of a holy one will be very full! But these aren't things that will simply keep you busy. These commands become natural parts of the lifestyle of the believer.

How do you live every day? Is your daily life like your church life? Do you act, feel, and speak in a godly way on a daily basis? Is your life consistently holy? God desires His children to be holy like Him. His holiness is eternal. Our holiness should be a daily evidence of our commitment to Him.

DEDICATED

In order to be consistent in our holy living, the believer must be dedicated—dedicated to the Lord and dedicated to living for Him daily.

Do you know someone who is dedicated—truly devoted? List that person's name here and describe some behaviors that would document her dedication. _____

_____

_____

My precious mother-in-law is totally dedicated. She is completely sold out to Jesus and gives her whole self to Him. She is unwavering in her devotion to her husband and children. And she is also a wholehearted, dedicated sports fan. When her Houston Astros baseball team struggles in the national playoffs, she has faith that they will win. Even when her Baylor Bears football team trails many points behind, she never gives up. She believes they can win. Christians are to *never give up* in our pursuit of holiness. God calls us to be dedicated to holy living. Daily holiness results from true dedication to the Lord.

Hannah dedicated her long-awaited son, Samuel, to the Lord.

Read her heart-warming story in 1 Samuel 1:1–2:21.

She obediently gave her child to God—the ultimate sacrifice for a loving mother. Leaving her child in the temple to serve the Lord, Hannah prayed to the holy God on behalf of her child. Her heart's desire was to be faithful and raise a son who was faithful. Hannah's sacrificial devotion was a testimony to young Samuel and has been an example for Christian mothers through the years. Samuel himself lived a holy life—a judge and prophet in Israel whose spiritual leadership turned that nation back to God. Hannah's dedication to holiness brought blessings to herself and her offspring. Her devotion to God has blessed believers throughout generations. Are you willing to be dedicated like Hannah—giving up what you love most to be obedient, to be holy?

A believer must practice spiritual disciplines in order to live a holy life. Holiness does not come naturally. It is not easy. It takes effort and persistence. Discipline in holiness is necessary every day. *Discipline* is "training that corrects, molds, or perfects the mental faculties, or moral character." Holiness requires control and effort—it doesn't just happen.

Christians have the power of God as an added source to their own self-control. I call that "divine discipline," Spirit-controlled discipline of one-self, God's power plus my power. If God convicts you of a need for more personal discipline, you may benefit from reading my testimony in *Divine Discipline: How to Develop and Maintain Self-Control*. Personal and spiritual discipline is necessary for the believer to live a holy life. Let's consider the spiritual disciplines that are essential to holiness.

What are some spiritual disciplines that you believe a Christian should practice in order to be holy? List several specific disciplines below.

_____

_____

_____

_____

Daily discipline is essential to spiritual growth and maturity in the believer's life. Increased knowledge of God and persistent obedience should result in holiness. If that is true, spiritual discipline and holy living are dependent upon each other. Let's take time to discuss several spiritual disciplines: Bible study, prayer, fellowship, service, witnessing, and meditation. While this is not an exhaustive list of spiritual disciplines, these spiritual disciplines are necessary for daily holiness.

1. Bible Study

Most Christians believe and love the Bible, but so few actually study it. Personal, in-depth Bible study is essential for spiritual growth and daily holiness. The Bible makes us aware of sin and helps us live godly lives (Ps. 119:9–11; Heb. 5:12–14). Do you spend time daily studying the Bible? Are you disciplined in the study of His Word? Do you know more about the Bible today than when you came to faith in Him? It's not too late to begin or resume your daily Bible study.

Make a plan and stick with it so you can develop daily holiness.

_____

_____

_____

2. Prayer

Spiritual discipline includes daily prayer, as well as regular Bible study. Conversation with the Father not only strengthens your relationship with Him, a spirit of prayer also promotes holiness. In order to keep prayer a priority in your life, set a time and place for prayer. Select some prayer resources such as books on prayer and keep a prayer list or prayer journal. How long has it been since you prayed? How long did you pray?

Set some goals to develop the daily discipline of prayer.

_____

_____

3. Fellowship

Biblical fellowship is the bonding together or joining together of those devoted to God. Fellowship or communion with God through prayer and Bible study builds your relationship with Him. The more fellowship the tighter the bond. We are also to have fellowship with God's church and His children. Regular participation in worship and attendance in church strengthen the relationship with God too. It is not always easy or desirable to attend church, but corporate worship strengthens your faith. Believers also benefit from fellowship with other believers. Fellowship promotes daily holiness. My husband says that "Christians are like bananas—they grow best in bundles." So be actively involved in fellowship with other believers.

4. Service

A disciplined believer will be involved in serving others. The servant spirit of Jesus was reflected in His unending ministry to others. Believers who are growing in the Lord daily should desire to serve others willingly and unselfishly. But ministry takes time and effort. It is worth it though because of earthly blessings and eternal rewards. Ministry begins with your family and continues with your neighbors and even strangers. Are you involved in ministry to others? How do you serve others? Discipline yourself to serve faithfully as Jesus did every day.

5. Witnessing

One of the toughest spiritual disciplines is witnessing or evangelism. While most Christians believe evangelism should be a priority for the church, few actually witness. Christians must discipline themselves daily to be witnesses. Discipline is necessary for believers to talk about their faith. My husband, Chuck, who is an evangelism professor, says, "Witnessing should be the natural result of a heart warmed in the presence of God, a life that resembles the life of Jesus, and a genuine concern for other people." Is your heart on fire for God? Is your life a testimony of Him? Are you burdened for lost people you know? Discipline your heart and your life and you can become a daily witness.

6. Meditation

Even the world today recognizes the benefit of meditation. World religions and yoga recommend regular periods of meditation for their followers to reduce stress and get in tune with their spirits. God was the first person to recommend meditation to His followers. Meditation for the believer is focusing thoughts on God, listening to Him, thinking about His teachings, being still in His presence. Joshua 1:8 says, *"This Book of the Law shall not depart from your mouth, but you shall meditate in it day and night, in that you may observe to do according to all that is written in it. For then you will make your way prosperous, and then you will have good success."* Strength and power come to the believer in times of meditation. Holy living is a natural result of daily meditation on God and His Word. The psalmist gave instruction about meditation: *"His delight is in the law of the Lord, and in His law he meditates day and night"* (Ps. 1:2).

The life of holiness does not simply come from desire. Holy living results only when the believer makes a *daily* commitment to be *dedicated* to the Lord and *disciplined* in godliness. What a challenge! Athletes face this challenge as they train for the Olympics. They must practice their sport daily, be dedicated wholeheartedly, and be disciplined in training. Then they can compete and may even win. Believers face this challenge as we run this race called life. We must live for the Lord daily; be dedicated wholeheartedly to Him; and be disciplined in spiritual matters. Then we can successfully compete and will win an eternal reward.

Write and memorize the Scripture verse at the beginning of the chapter._____

_____

_____

You will not be able to succeed in daily holiness without dedication and discipline.

**List below a specific goal in each spiritual discipline.
Then commit these plans to the Lord.**

    1. Bible study _____

    2. Prayer _____

    3. Fellowship _____

    4. Service _____

    5. Witnessing _____

You will achieve daily holiness as you practice these spiritual disciplines *daily*!

EPHESIANS
4:24

"You must display a new nature because you are a new person, created in God's likeness—righteous, holy, and true."

Habits are behaviors which shape a character. They can strengthen or weaken a person. That is why there has been extensive teaching about habits throughout history. At the turn of the twentieth century, Samuel Smiles said:

Sow a thought and you reap an act;
Sow an act and you reap a habit;
Sow a habit and you reap a character;
Sow a character and you reap a destiny.

Now at the turn of the twenty-first century, we can echo his truths. Many bad thoughts lead to unholy habits. And those unholy habits result in a very ungodly world. It is encouraging to realize that good thoughts can lead to holy habits, and holy habits can shape our character and change the world.

What is a habit? Write your personal definition here. _____

_____

_____

Many people think a habit is bad manners or irritating behavior like cracking your knuckles or chewing with your mouth open. Others think a habit is something you do unconsciously, without thinking, like cracking your knuckles or smacking your lips. But a habit is actually a much broader behavior, a more general action. A *habit* is defined as a manner of conducting oneself or a settled tendency or usual manner of behavior. More specifically, a *habit* is a behavior pattern acquired by frequent repetition that has become nearly or completely involuntary.

With those definitions in mind, what are some of your own personal habits? Are those habits good or bad, holy or unholy?

In his book *The Pursuit of Holiness*, Jerry Bridges identifies four principles about holiness. These practical lessons will help us understand why believers must develop holy habits. The first principle is that habits are developed and reinforced by frequent repetition. Anything that is done over and over will become a habit. Saying no to sin over and over again results in holy habits. The second principle is never let an exception occur. If you allow an exception for sin, you reinforce the old habits of ungodliness. The third principle is that diligence in all areas is required to ensure success in one area. A believer must energetically pursue holiness in all aspects of life. And the last principle is don't be discouraged by failure. Sinful nature causes failures in holy living, but God forgives and restores a believer who keeps on trying to live a holy life and develop holy habits.

Paul wrote about the habits of the old man and new man in his letter to the Christians in Ephesus. Many of the less mature believers had failed to develop new godly habits of behavior. Though converted, they were continuing their old sinful habits. Paul confronted them directly, criticizing their ungodly behavior and characterizing their desired godly lifestyles.

Read Ephesians 4:17–32. Then write a descriptive contrast between the old man in sin and the new man in Christ. _____

_____

_____

_____

_____

OLD HABITS, NEW HABITS

Believers are no longer to live the sinful lifestyle of the old life. Instead the believer is to develop new thought patterns and behaviors—holy habits. Intimacy with God should replace alienation from God. Wisdom should replace ignorance. Clear knowledge of God's will should replace blindness by sin.

The Christians in Ephesus had become lewd, unclean, and greedy. God, through Jesus Christ, forgave their sin and made each of them a new creation—a *holy* being, not just a human being. As a result they stopped lying, stealing, nagging, and blaming. They started loving, encouraging, and forgiving. Those Christians developed some holy habits. We need to begin today to repeat those thoughts and actions which can become holy habits—evidence of the new creation in Christ.

Read the following Scriptures and fill in the blanks to list some of the holy habits that believers should develop through frequent repetition.

1. Be confident in the _____ of God. Measure all thoughts against Scripture (Ps. 119:160).

2. Always tell the _____. Do not _____ or distort the truth (Lev. 19:11).

3. Do not be angry or impatient. Be _____ and patient (1 Cor. 13:4–5).

4. Use _____ language in all your conversation. Let your word be clean and positive (Eph. 4:29).

5. Think pure _____ . Put away sinful ideas (Phil. 4:8).

6. Be consistent morally. Screen reading material, television, and movies for _____ content (1 Cor. 6:18) .

7. _____ others in words and deeds. Put the needs of others before your own (1 Thess. 5:11).

8. Be _____, not negative and critical, in your attitude and actions (Jas. 5:9).

9. Stand up for what you believe. Be _____ in your faith (Eph. 6:10).

10. Be _____ where you go and what you do. You are always a witness (Eph. 5:15).

11. Work _____ with your hands. Be diligent and productive (Prov. 10:4).

12. Make _____ and Bible study a natural part of your day (1 Thess. 5:17).

13. _____ Scripture and meditate on the Word, applying it to your life (Ps. 119:11).

14. Embody the ten commandments. _____ God and His Word (Deut. 27:10).

15. Be constantly in a state of _____. Praise and pray without ceasing (Ps. 2:11).

16. Be faithful in church attendance and service. _____ with other believers (Acts 2:42).

17. Practice the presence of God throughout the day. God is _____ with you (Matt. 28:20).

18. Be a good _____. Care for those around you (Gal. 5:14).

19. Bear witness of God's work in your life. Share a word of _____ (2 Tim. 1:8).

20. Be kind and _____ in all your relationships. God loves through you (Matt. 5:43–45).

21. Practice the golden rule. Do unto _____ as you would have them do unto _____ (Matt. 7:12).

22. Be _____, sharing all that you have with others (1 Tim. 6:18).

23. Be self-controlled in your thoughts and actions. Your _____ will be a testimony (Col. 2:5).

24. _____ others freely and unconditionally as God so freely _____ you (Eph. 4:32).

25. Be _____ with others and serve them because of your _____ (Phil. 2:17–18).

Samuel Johnson once said that the chains of habit are too weak to be felt until they are too strong to be broken. Are you developing some holy habits that are growing too strong to be broken? As your holy habits strengthen your faith, you will not only *grow* but also you will *go* on living for the Lord. You will remain holy in this unholy world!

HOLY SCRIPTURES FOR HOLY LIVING

Write and memorize the Scripture verse at the beginning of the chapter. _____

_____

_____

PERSONAL HOLINESS

Has God convicted you of some ungodly habits? Has He challenged you to develop some new godly habits? Be specific as you list them below.

Old Habits _____

_____

_____

New Habits _____

_____

_____

Claim God's promise in Ephesians 4:24 that He can create in you a new person of true righteousness and holiness.

HEBREWS 12:14

"Pursue peace with all people, and holiness, without which no one will see the Lord."

Holiness is not a status to be achieved, but a life goal to be pursued. Because we are human, no man or woman can ever be holy like God. Every believer, however, should pursue holiness. Pursuit requires effort and hard work. Pursuit implies a lifelong task. Pursuit demands discipline but results in difference—a different life.

Hebrews 12:14 says to pursue peace with all people and holiness, without which no one will see God. When believers have an active and growing relationship with God, their pursuit of holiness will be a vital part of living.

Read Hebrews 12:14 in several translations. Write the verse in your own words as you decide to pursue holiness. _____

_____

_____

_____

_____

Pursue, strive for, seek, work toward holiness. Our challenge as believers is to become more holy every day.

The prophet Isaiah proclaimed the holiness of God and challenged the children of God to be holy. In Isaiah 6, the holiness of God was announced in the temple and the holiness of God was to be lived out in His people. Isaiah gave a visual image that helps us understand how we must pursue holiness.

Read Isaiah 6:1–8. Underline the threefold holy and any other words that describe the holiness of God.

Can you picture the temple with the Lord sitting high up on His throne? While our Holy God reigns from His throne in heaven, He also reigns over the world and in our lives. Around the temple, there were seraphim (fiery creatures with six wings) guarding the holiness of God. As the seraphim positioned their wings, they instructed God's children in the pursuit of holiness.

Reread Isaiah 6:2. How were the wings of the seraphim positioned? Complete the following phrases:

    with two wings they covered their   _____
    with two wings they covered their   _____
    with two wings they   _____

The placement of their wings symbolizes aspects of personal holiness. With two wings, the seraphim covered his face, indicating reverence. With two wings he covered his feet, depicting humility. And with two wings he flew, demonstrating service. The pursuit of holiness involves reverence, humility, and service. Let's examine each part of the pursuit.

The seraphim's first indication of the pursuit of holiness was the covering of his eyes in reverence. Those fiery creatures expressed respect for God as they hid their eyes.

FEAR GOD

Look up the word *reverence* in the dictionary to better understand this response. Write your definition here. _____
_____
_____
_____

Reverence is profound respect and love, awesome fear and dread. A believer's pursuit of holiness begins with total fear of God, not panic or dread but deep awe and respect. The Bible teaches that the fear of the Lord is the beginning of wisdom (Prov. 1:7) and that the consequences of sin should be feared (Prov. 28:1–4). What else does the Bible teach about the fear of the Lord?

Read the following verses and record a biblical teaching about the fear of God beside each reference.

Proverbs 2:5 _____

_____

Proverbs 9:10 _____

_____

Proverbs 14:26–27 _____

_____

Proverbs 15:33 _____

_____

Proverbs 22:4 _____

_____

The fear of God leads to an understanding of Him and His holiness (Prov. 2:5; 9:10). The fear of God gives confidence and life (Prov. 14:26-27). The fear of the Lord gives instruction and leads to humility (Prov. 15:33). And the fear of God results in blessings and honor (Prov. 22:4). Believers should be inspired by the Word to fear God.

Mary of Bethany demonstrated her fear of God when out of profound respect and deep love, she anointed the feet of Jesus with very costly oil (John 12:3).

How do you show respect to God? What are some specific ways you demonstrate your fear of God? _____

_____

_____

_____

_____

Do you relish God's presence? Do you bask in His love? Do you call out to Him in love? Do you seek His face? Do you honor His name? Those who truly respect God respect His person, His people, and His place. If you honestly desire to pursue holiness, you must fear God and commit yourself to Him. You must love Him with all your heart, and seek Him with all your soul. You must hold Him up and worship Him. Those who fear God will pursue Him and pursue holiness.

HUMBLE YOURSELF

The seraphim also depicted the importance of humility by covering their feet with two of their wings. While reverence is the first step in a believer's pursuit of holiness, humility is the natural next step. When a believer realizes who God is, she quickly realizes who she is not. Humility is a natural result of reverence.

The New Testament teaches that humility is total dependence on God and respect for others. Humility is not a weakness but a strength from God. Because human nature is selfish and proud, the pursuit of holiness demands unselfish humility. A believer must be humbled before a very holy God.

Humility is not a trait pursued by the world. In fact, the Greek world and our present world abhor the quality of humility. Humility is seen by the world as a sign of weakness and inferiority. Therefore, humility is a virtue that sets believers apart—makes us holy like Him.

Fill in the blanks below to indicate how God rewards the humble.

He puts down the mighty and _____ the lowly (Luke 1:52).

Humble yourselves in the sight of the Lord, and He will _____ you up (Jas. 4:10).

Humble yourselves under the mighty hand of God, that He may exalt you in _____ time (1 Pet. 5:6).

The Lord criticizes the proud and blesses the humble (Luke 1:52). He lifts up those who bow their knees before Him (Jas. 4:10). He exalts those who are humble in His own time (1 Pet. 5:6). While the world may not reward meekness and humility, God honors those believers who humble themselves in their pursuit of holiness.

The apostle Paul reflected on the humble spirit of a colaborer named Phoebe.

Read her brief story in Romans 16:1–2. Note Paul's accolades. How did he describe her? _____

_____

Phoebe, who humbly served the Lord and His church, was called by Paul *sister, servant, saint, helper*. Her humble service demonstrated her holiness and resulted in her praise. While the world does not recognize the humble, the Lord does.

With two of their wings, the seraphim covered their faces in reverence and with two wings they covered their feet in humility. With their last two wings the seraphim flew. We must learn to serve others as we pursue holiness. Service to others should be the natural result of a holy life.

Service in the Bible actually refers to joy in doing for others, in meeting their needs. Ministry and service put feet to a heart of holiness.

SERVE OTHERS

Circle each biblical teaching about service in the Scriptures below.

Matthew 20:28: *The Son of Man did not come to be served, but to serve, and to give His life a ransom for many.*

John 12:26: *If anyone serves Me, let him follow Me; and where I am, there My servant will be also. If anyone serves Me, him My Father will honor.*

Romans 12:11: *Not lagging in diligence, be fervent in spirit, serving the Lord.*

Galatians 5:13: *For you… have been called to liberty; only do not use liberty as an opportunity for the flesh, but through love serve one another.*

Ephesians 6:6–7: *As bondservants of Christ, doing the will of God from the heart, with goodwill doing service, as to the Lord, and not to men.*

Are you involved in service? Is your commitment to holiness being expressed through ministry to others? If so, you are being obedient to God's will for His people. If not, you need to renew a commitment to the pursuit of holiness and service to others. Make service to the Lord and service to others major life priorities.

Dorcas was a woman in the early church who reflected God's holiness in her life of service. The Scripture says, "*She was full of good works and charitable deeds which she did*" (Acts 9:36). Dorcas not only noticed the needs of those around her but also did something to meet those needs. Using her ability to sew, Dorcas made clothes for the widows in her hometown. Her ministry to them was so significant that the ladies grieved deeply when she died. God, through the apostle Peter, gave life back to Dorcas so she could continue serving others. Her consistent holiness was a lifestyle witness and her dedicated service was a life-changing ministry. Let Dorcas be an example of service for you.

Are you pursuing holiness? Is a life of holiness a daily commitment for you? How do you show your love and respect for God? Have you humbled yourself in total dependence upon God? Are you joyfully serving others? God who is Holy desires His children to be holy—holy as well as happy.

Holiness is not what God does but who God is. The pursuit of holiness for the believer should be the lifelong effort of becoming holy like God. Don't be focused on doing good, but becoming holy. Many believers get off track in their pursuit of holiness when they busy themselves *doing* and don't allow God to perfect His holiness in them.

Write and memorize the Scripture verse at the beginning of the chapter. _____
_____
_____

Take a moment to do a personal evaluation of your life in Christ. Are you pursuing holiness daily? Are you renewing your commitment to holy living every day? Do you feel you are making progress in your pursuit of holiness?

Give a specific example below of how your holiness is being reflected through reverence, humility, and service. How have you recently demonstrated your holiness? List some ways under these categories.

Fear of God _____
Humility of Self _____
Service to Others _____

Praise the Lord with the seraphim as you proclaim, "Holy, holy, holy is the Lord of hosts; The whole earth is full of His glory!" (Isa. 6:3).

ROMANS
6:22

"But now having been set free from sin, and having become slaves of God, you have your fruit to holiness, and the end, everlasting life."

While we shouldn't be holy just to receive rewards, we do receive blessings for our holiness. Believers should ask the questions, *What is the evidence of holiness in our lives? What is the fruit of holiness?* In the answers to these questions are often the blessings of offering our holiness in an unholy world.

Scripture speaks a lot about fruit, not just the edible kind. *Fruit* is first introduced in Genesis when God created the grass and trees. He specified that the fruit tree yields fruit according to its own kind (Gen. 1:11). Fruit is the product of the specific tree. This basic biblical principle teaches that the type of tree affects the product of the tree. Thus a holy life will produce holy fruit.

Later in Genesis it was the fruit eaten by Adam and Eve that brought sin into the world (Gen. 3:6). The fruit or harvest of the land was given as an offering to the Lord (Gen. 4:3). Children were called the fruit of the womb, a blessing from God (Gen. 30:2). The Psalms speak often of fruit as evidences of a godly life (Pss. 1:3; 92:14; 104:13). The Proverbs also refer to fruit as the works of God (Prov. 8:19; 11:30). The prophets describe the fruit or the results of their doings (Is. 3:10; Jer. 6:19; Ezek. 17:8-9; Dan. 4:20-22; Hos. 10:1,13; Amos 6:12). The Old Testament is filled with references about fruit.

In the New Testament, *fruit* most often refers to the work of the Holy Spirit in a believer's life (Gal. 5:22-23). Fruit is a result of righteousness

(Phil. 1:11; Jas. 3:18) and a picture of new believers (Rom. 1:13; 1 Cor. 16:15). Fruit may sometimes communicate that sense of reward or blessing (John 4:36; Phil. 4:17).

Examine the Scriptures above. What do you understand the word _fruit_ to mean in the Bible? Write your ideas here. _____

_____

_____

_____

_____

The fruit of the Holy Spirit is a wonderful study. If you haven't personally examined this biblical teaching, I encourage you to do so. You could simply study the primary passage in Galatians 5:22–25. Or you could complete a more in-depth study available in your local Christian bookstore. But for the purposes of our study of personal holiness, let's focus on what the Bible says about the rewards of holiness.

Before we investigate other fruit of holiness, take a few moments to consider evidences of holiness in your own life. As you think of them, list how you have demonstrated the fruit of the Spirit mentioned in Galatians 5.

	Fruit of the Spirit (Gal. 5:22–23)	**Fruit of Holiness** (My Life)
Love	_____	_____
Joy	_____	_____
Peace	_____	_____
Patience	_____	_____
Kindness	_____	_____
Goodness	_____	_____
Faithfulness	_____	_____
Gentleness	_____	_____
Self-Control	_____	_____

In her Bible study _Living Beyond Yourself_, Beth Moore says that while the fruit of the Holy Spirit—love, joy, peace, patience, kindness, goodness, faithfulness, gentleness, and self-control—is living proof that the Spirit of God dwells in you, the Bible also teaches about other fruit of holiness. Now let's consider a few of the blessings of the holy life.

A primary fruit of holiness is _joy_—not just happiness or pleasure. Joy is a profound sense of excitement that results from knowing and serving God. It is truly the fruit or blessing of a right relationship with God. Those who

JOY

live holy lives experience true joy. Joy also encourages holiness. Jerry Bridges, author of *The Pursuit of Holiness*, said, "Joy not only results from a holy life, but there is also a sense in which joy helps produce a holy life."

Do you believe that joy is a fruit of holiness? If so, write the word joy in the statement below.

God gives abundant _____ to those who obediently follow Him and live holy lives.

Jesus Himself said that joy would be given to those who obey Him (John 15:10–11). Thus, only those who are pursuing holiness as a way of life will receive abundant joy from God the Father.

Think about joy—true joy. What kind of life produces true joy?
_____
_____

Would you receive greater joy from living a sinful life or a holy life?_____

Why? _____
_____
_____
_____

God clearly calls His children to live holy lives, and He rewards the righteous for their goodness. Abundant blessings are experienced by those who live holy lives. Are you filled with the joy of the Lord? If not, you may not be walking in holiness. Sin can rob you of your joy (Ps. 51:8,12). Joy will return when the believer walks in holiness.

WISDOM

Another fruit of holiness is *wisdom*. Wisdom is generally thought to be accumulated learning, discernment, or good sense. The Bible says wisdom is from God and that God is all-knowing (omniscient) or wise. As children of God make godly choices and live holy lives, God gives them wisdom to know Him and His will.

James 3:13–18 contrasts heavenly wisdom and demonic wisdom or wisdom from God and wisdom from the devil. Read this passage and list some differences between heavenly wisdom and earthly wisdom.

Heavenly Wisdom	Earthly Wisdom
_____	_____
_____	_____
_____	_____
_____	_____
_____	_____
_____	_____

While God gives heavenly wisdom to those who obey Him, the devil offers earthly wisdom to those who live by their own desires. Those who are truly wise show good conduct (v. 13) and sow the fruit of righteousness (v. 18). As believers make wise decisions, they develop holy lifestyles. And as believers live out God's holiness, they become wiser. Wisdom is evident when a believer leads a life marked by purity, peace, gentleness, a yielding spirit, good fruits without partiality and hypocrisy. In other words, a believer's holiness is a sign of wisdom.

Let's discuss one more fruit of holiness—freedom. Freedom is the absence of bondage; it is total liberation. As a believer lives a holy life, there is great freedom. The believer is no longer enslaved to sin but free in Christ. Holiness does lead to freedom.

In the Book of Romans, Paul wrote about death to sin, and life in Christ. Then in chapter 6, the apostle used the analogy of slavery to help the Christian understand that a sinful life leads to bondage and a righteous life leads to freedom.

Read Romans 6:22 and write its meaning in your own words.

_____

_____

_____

_____

Salvation is delivery not only from the *penalty* of sin but also from the *power* of sin. When a believer professes faith in Jesus Christ, a holy life should result. The gift of God for salvation is eternal life—the fruit of salvation is holiness and the fruit of holiness is freedom. It is freedom from the penalty of sin and freedom to pursue holiness.

In his book *The Way of Holiness*, Stephen Olford talks about the different ways the fruit of holiness is evidenced in a believer's life. If you are truly living a holy life, you should bear fruit or yield a harvest in every area of your life including your worship, your walk, and your work. How fruitful are you? Are you releasing the Spirit in your life? Have you grown closer to God in your daily life?

FREEDOM

Rate your personal fruitfulness in each of these areas. On a scale from 1 to 5, with 1 being the lowest and 5 the highest, circle a number below that honestly reflects your fruitfulness in...

Your Christian Worship	1	2	3	4	5
Your Christian Walk	1	2	3	4	5
Your Christian Work	1	2	3	4	5

As you conclude this study on the fruit of holiness, reflect on the fruit you bear and rejoice in the fruitfulness of others.

HOLY SCRIPTURE FOR HOLY LIVING

Write and memorize the Scripture verse at the beginning of the chapter. _____
_____
_____

PERSONAL HOLINESS

List the fruit of holiness in your life. Thank God for the evidence of His work in your life!
_____
_____
_____

Now pray for God to convict you of your need to bear more fruit of holiness.

What works of the Holy Spirit do you desire to develop in your life?
_____
_____
_____
_____

God wants you to bear the fruit of holiness. He can do it through you!

PSALM 111:9

"He has sent redemption to His people; He has commanded His covenant forever; Holy and awesome is His name."

In a very ungodly world, the believer often feels hopeless in the task of reaching the world for Christ. However, we must not be discouraged but be even more committed to live holy lives. We need to understand that even one godly person can have a powerful influence. After all, it took only one river to carve the Grand Canyon.

St. John Chrysostom said, "If but ten among us lead a holy life, we shall kindle a fire which shall light up the entire city." Because of the power of the Holy Spirit, even a few believers can have a profound influence in this ungodly world. Your holy life counts; it counts for eternity!

Influence is the power exerted over the minds or behavior of others. It can be a spiritual or moral force, a positive or negative power, or a godly or ungodly witness. People can truly have influence on other people. The greatest influence on a believer's life should be Jesus Christ—His perfect life and His power to save. Women of the Bible can also be a powerful influence on Christian women today. Many godly women throughout history have had great impact on others. Women have the real ability to influence others to God and holy living.

What woman has had a profound influence on your life? _____

_____

Why? _____

_____

How has her influence affected your life? _____

_____

God calls each of us to be an influence in our world, our church, our community, and our family. We cannot have a godly influence without living a holy life. Words alone do not make a godly impact; it takes a holy life. You have the power to determine whether your influence will be for good or for evil. Let's consider the power of holiness as you make a commitment to influence others to witness, to serve, and to love.

While Jesus Christ alone has the power to save, He has given His children the power to witness to others about Him. You yourself must be a witness, and you must encourage others to be a witness through their words and deeds. In Matthew 28:19-20, when Jesus gave the Great Commission, His challenge to go and witness was for all Christians. Christian women can be powerful witnesses in their homes, their communities, and the world. But you must ask God to give you His power to witness.

What does the Bible teach about the power to witness? _____

_____

_____

_____

Read the following Scripture passages and summarize a biblical truth about witnessing. Scripture can empower you in your witness.

1 John 1:3 _____

Galatians 6:8–9 _____

Acts 1:8 _____

2 Corinthians 6:17 _____

1 Peter 3:15 _____

Psalm 51:13 _____

1 Thessalonians 5:17 _____

2 Timothy 1:7 _____

In order to be a witness, a believer must have fellowship with Jesus Christ through a personal faith relationship (1 John 1:3). Secondly, a believer must have a love for others and a passion for the lost to be saved (Ps. 126:6).

In addition, believers must be willing to share the gospel with the whole world (Acts 1:8). A holy life, separated from the world, gives power to a believer's witness (2 Cor. 6:17), and a word of witness brings salvation (1 Pet. 3:15). A study of the Bible prepares the witness (Ps. 51:13), and unceasing prayer enables the witness (1 Thess. 5:17). God does not give fear to the believer. He gives power to witness (2 Tim. 1:7). The word of testimony plus a holy lifestyle give a believer the power to witness. It is this witness that is the influence of holiness.

POWER TO SERVE

The Holy Spirit gives us the power to witness and the power to serve. It is often service to others, specific acts of kindness, that influences an unbeliever to faith in Jesus Christ. A kind deed done in the name of Jesus can influence others to salvation and to holy living. While service is not necessary for salvation, service is an evidence of salvation. It is faith that saves, although works are a natural result of a right relationship with God.

In a final teaching to His disciples, Jesus discussed the judgment.

Read Matthew 25:31–46 to identify what determines how God will judge His people. _____

_____

_____

_____

_____

_____

Salvation is based on faith alone, although the final judgment will be determined in part by the believer's treatment of others. Jesus said the sheep are those who serve others while the goats are those who serve self. Christ will separate the sheep from the goats. He will reward those who serve others in His name. Your acts of kindness do not go unnoticed by God.

Review Matthew 25:31–46 again to identify specific ways to serve others. What is the personal need and how can you respond?

Their Need	My Response
hungry	_____
thirsty	_____
stranger	_____
naked	_____
sick	_____
imprisoned	_____

Who in your community has these needs?

_____

_____

Jesus challenges the believer to minister to others, but the Holy Spirit empowers us to serve. As you meet the needs of others, you are ministering to Jesus Himself. Often unselfish service gives your word of witness a voice—service influences others to holiness.

Jesus Christ gives to each believer the power to witness and the power to serve. He also gives to every believer the power to love. Love is definitely from God. Not only is God by His very nature love, but also He is the source of love. Love is God and love comes from God. Love expressed in words and actions definitely has the power to influence others. Your love can influence others to love.

Let's take a few moments to examine what the Scripture teaches about love, especially the power of love to change people. The story of the Samaritan woman recorded in John 4 summarizes the power of love. Jesus, in love, reached out to this sinful woman who had come to the well for water. He knew she needed more than water. She needed His love and eternal life. Because of His loving concern for her need, the woman accepted His gift of salvation. He not only gave her His unconditional love but also gave her the ability to love others.

Read John 4:27–30 to see the power of God's love in the life of the Samaritan woman. What happened as a result of her love for others?

_____

_____

_____

_____

Scripture records that this forgiven woman immediately began to tell others about Christ, and they were saved. Her personal testimony was a natural result of Christ's love for her and her love for others. Love motivates the believer to witness and serve. Love influences others to salvation and to holiness.

What is your personal testimony? What has God been doing in your life? How has God demonstrated His love to you? Write a brief testimony here and pray that God will use your testimony to influence others to Him.

_____

_____

_____

_____

_____

_____

God has given you the power to witness, to serve, and to love. His power can have a profound influence on people. His name alone can change the human heart and develop a holy life.

There is great power and influence in a name. My grandfather often reminded his young grandchildren to honor the family's name. He warned us that our actions could either strengthen or destroy the family's name. This is so true. A person's misbehavior can tarnish the family's name or her good conduct can honor the family's name. As Christians, our actions can also bring glory and honor or embarrassment and shame to our Father's name. A person's name can generate respect or ridicule based upon personal behavior. Reflect on the scorn shown toward Christianity when a believer stumbles in her faith or engages in immorality.

God desires for His name to be honored. The psalmist praised the greatness of God when he said, *"Holy and awesome is His name"* (Ps. 111:9). God's name alone communicates love and respect.

Scripture also tells us that at the name of Jesus *"every knee should bow...and every tongue should confess that Jesus Christ is Lord, to the glory of God the Father"* (Phil. 2:10-11). There is power in the name of Jesus—power to save and power to change. That is why the holy life of a believer can influence others to Him. God's power to save and change is reflected through the holy lives of His children. Your one holy life can change the world!

HOLY SCRIPTURE FOR HOLY LIVING

Write and memorize the Scripture verse at the beginning of the chapter._____

_____

_____

PERSONAL HOLINESS

What influence have you had on others? Has your one life made a difference for Him? Think of a person who has been influenced by you through your witness, your service, or your love. Write their names below.

    My Witness _____

_____

    My Service _____

_____

    My Love _____

_____

Pray that God will continue to use you as an influence of holiness.

REVELATION
4:8

*"Holy, holy, holy, Lord God Almighty,
Who was and is and is to come."*

Now that we have studied what the Bible teaches about holiness, it is necessary for us to talk about the permanency of holiness. The Bible clearly states that God always has been and always will be holy. *"Holy, holy, holy, Lord God Almighty; Who was and is and is to come"* (Rev. 4:8). His holiness is unchanging. He desires us to continue in holiness. He wants our holiness to be unchanging, to last forever—the longevity of holiness. If you believe that God's holiness is eternal and everlasting, then as a believer you must seek to maintain a holy lifestyle forever. That's the challenge in this unholy world!

It's easy for almost anyone to be holy for a moment, to be good for a time, to be godly while at church. The tough part of the Christian life is continuing in the faith and being holy day after day.

Is it hard for you to be persistent in living a holy life? Have you started to practice holy talking or holy actions and then stopped? Have you given up some bad habits to be more holy, then without even realizing it resumed those ungodly behaviors? List any commitments to holiness that you have made and broken.

Read Galatians 6:9 and 1 Corinthians 15:58 for encouragement. Now ask God's forgiveness. Then renew your commitment to continue in holiness for the rest of your life.

Let's consider the longevity of holiness. How long *does* and *should* holiness last? If we are speaking of the holiness of God, the answer is simple—God's holiness is eternal. But if we are considering human holiness, the answer is much more complex. Humans must develop holiness before it can be sustained. Sinful human nature makes the consistency of holiness difficult. But by the Holy Spirit's power, any obedient believer can develop and maintain a holy life. Holiness by God's standard should last *a long time*. It should last for your lifetime as you daily recommit to holiness; it should last for your family's lifetime as you pass down a heritage of holiness; and it should last for all eternity as you experience glorification in the presence of God.

Holiness should last for a lifetime if it is genuine, if it is growing, and if it is glorifying God. Stephen Olford said, "Given spiritual life, holiness means the maintaining in health of that life before God and the setting apart of that life for His service alone." Though difficult and against human nature, holiness can last as you maintain that commitment to God every day of your life.

Read Revelation 4:1–11. Do you note some similarities between Isaiah's proclamation of the holiness of God and this proclamation by John? _____

_____

_____

_____

_____

Both passages talk about the glory and holiness of God. Both passages involve creatures in the proclamation. Both passages depict God on the throne. Both passages speak the word *holy* three times to stress its importance and longevity. These threefold proclamations also parallel the Trinity—Father, Son, and Holy Spirit.

In John's description of the throne of heaven, one can begin to imagine the glory and holiness of God. God's glory and holiness are everlasting.

What specific words or phrases depict the longevity of God's holiness? _____

_____

_____

_____

John reinforced the longevity of God's holiness three times when he said they do not rest (v. 8), day and night (v. 8), and forever and ever (v. 10).

How can you maintain a holy life without resting, day and night, forever and ever? In one of his New Testament epistles, this same Apostle John gave directives for a lifetime of holiness. In 1 John 2:15–17, believers are warned not to love the world but to love God, not to long for the world but to desire God, not to live in the flesh but to follow the will of God. What a formula for lifelong holiness: love God, desire God, follow God. If you can make that commitment daily, then your holiness will last for a lifetime. In the same way, the creatures in Revelation 4:8–11 never stopped proclaiming the holiness of God, we should never stop living a holy life—without resting, day and night, forever and ever.

LASTING FOR YOUR FAMILY'S LIFETIME

Holiness should last for your lifetime, but it should also be passed down through your family. There is no greater legacy than that of a holy life! Christian women have the command to be holy and the responsibility to teach holiness to others. The home is the perfect place for a lifestyle of holiness to be imitated and instructed. Wives, mothers, grandmothers, sisters, and aunts can pass along a spiritual heritage of holiness. On the other hand, if you are not maintaining holy living, your family will be less likely to develop and maintain holiness. An ungodly walk is obvious first to your family. You should be motivated to persevere in holiness for your own sake and the sake of your family.

The story of Lois and Eunice is an inspiring reminder of the power of a godly woman to influence her family to holiness.

Read 2 Timothy 1:3–5. How did Lois and Eunice teach young Timothy about holiness? _____
_____
_____
_____
_____
_____

Timothy was grateful for the godly instruction of his grandmother Lois and his mother Eunice who taught him about faith, explained the Holy Scripture, and helped him increase in wisdom (see also 2 Tim. 3:15).

Are you grateful for the godly examples of your family? _____
What is your heritage of holiness? _____
_____
_____

Think of your own family tree. On the next page, fill in the names of those who passed along their faith and commitment to holiness.

Grandfather _____

Grandmother _____

Grandfather _____

Grandmother _____

Paternal Aunts/Uncles

_____

_____

_____

_____

Father _____

Mother _____

Maternal Aunts/Uncles

_____

_____

_____

_____

Sisters

_____

_____

_____

_____

Brothers

_____

_____

_____

_____

You _____

If you do not have a heritage of godly relatives, thank God that He has brought you into a relationship with Him.

Pray for family members who do not know God. Briefly record how you will strive to change the heritage for those who come in generations after you. _____

_____

_____

_____

_____

Like Timothy, I am blessed with a godly heritage. My mother and both grandmothers were examples of holiness for me. I have a sister and aunts who are committed Christians. When I married, I inherited a godly family, a mother-in-law and four sisters-in-law who are dedicated believers. Of course, I should also mention all the men in my family who have continued our legacy of holiness. In full-time ministry and as committed laymen, the godly men in my family have influenced me. Now it is my turn to continue my family's heritage of faith. I have the responsibility of passing the faith and holiness down to our future generations.

Timothy had the responsibility to continue his personal holiness and to pass along that commitment to others. Paul affirmed the faith of Lois and Eunice, which was passed along to Timothy and in turn passed along to many others. Paul said, *"The churches were strengthened in the faith, and increased in number daily"* (Acts 16:5).

You, too, have the opportunity and responsibility to pass your faith and holiness along to others. If you don't, holiness will not last for your family's lifetime.

To whom are you teaching faith and modeling holiness?_____

_____

Please name a few family members and friends whom you are influencing for God and godliness. _____

_____

_____

_____

You will be a factor in the longevity of your family's holiness. You can be the torchbearer lighting the flame of holiness for the next generation. Holiness can be an heirloom passed along to future generations in your family.

For the believer, holiness lasts not only for a lifetime but for all eternity. Holy living on earth is simply practice for an eternity of holiness with God in heaven. If the Christian doesn't enjoy being godly and seeking to be like God while alive on earth, that same Christian will be miserable in heaven where holiness is the norm not the exception. Can you imagine living in a place filled with only holy people for all eternity? What joy and satisfaction!

In Lesson Two, we discussed three doctrinal truths that explain salvation: *justification, sanctification, and glorification*. Do you remember the definitions? Lets review. *Justification* is experienced when a believer receives Jesus Christ as Savior and is saved from the penalty of sin that is death. *Sanctification* occurs during the believer's life as spiritual growth takes place and she is saved from the power of sin and enabled to live a holy life. *Glorification* comes after death when a believer becomes perfect like Christ and is saved from the presence of sin. It is in glorification that the believer's holiness can truly be complete and continue forever.

Let's take a few minutes to examine what a key Scripture teaches about glorification—that state of perfect holiness. Then we will learn how to continue growing in holiness until we are in the presence of God.

Read 1 Corinthians 15:50–58 and note at least three important truths about glorification. _____

_____

_____

_____

_____

What a joy to know that as a believer, one day I will be changed, incorruptible, and immortal in the presence of God! Death will be swallowed up by victory (1 Cor. 15:54). That promise gives comfort to us personally. The believer who dies is certainly in a better place and in a better state—with our Lord Jesus Christ, in perfect holiness.

It is exciting for a believer to consider being perfect like the Lord! In fact, it is somewhat unbelievable considering our sinfulness here on earth. But God promises that upon our death or His return, we will be perfect like Him and in the presence of Him in heaven.

What do you think of when you envision heaven? Describe heaven in your own words here. _____

_____

_____

_____

You probably used many wonderful adjectives to describe the beauty of heaven, but don't forget the people of heaven. God, the Holy One, will be sitting on His throne with all the heavenly hosts around Him. Believers from across the ages will enjoy fellowship with the Father. And you, dear believer, will be in the midst of them, in your most holy state, to spend all eternity.

Yes, the Bible tells us about heaven—the place prepared by God for all believers (John 14:3). The Bible teaches that heaven is a place without sorrow or sin. In heaven there will be no tears and no pain. (Read Revelation 21:1–7 for a true glimpse of heaven.) And in heaven, for the first time in our lives, we will be like Christ—perfect in every way. We will live in His presence forever. But heaven and glorification come later. For the believer, it is most important to develop holiness now.

The key to longevity in holiness is perseverance. Perseverance is the ability to continue—to go on living a holy life, day after day. Once you have committed to holy living, you must make a daily recommitment to holiness. As Paul concluded in 1 Corinthians 15, you must be *steadfast, immovable, always abounding in the work of the Lord, knowing that your labor is not in vain in the Lord"* (1 Cor. 15:58). If you continue in holiness, then you will be able to stand before the Lord in heaven knowing that you have grown in your likeness of Him. And at that moment, you will truly be like Him! Holiness is a Christian virtue worthy of sustaining and worthy of proclaiming.

HOLY SCRIPTURE FOR HOLY LIVING

Write and memorize the Scripture verse at the beginning of the chapter._____
_____
_____

PERSONAL HOLINESS

God's plan for the believer is a life of holiness that will last. How long has holiness lasted in your life and in your family? How long will you live a holy life? Reflect on your own life and the lives of your family members.

Write a one-sentence testimony or commitment of the longevity of your holiness.

_____
_____
_____
_____
_____

As you write, renew your commitment to be steadfast and immovable in your holiness.
My Lifetime of Holiness _____

My Family's Lifetime of Holiness _____

My Eternal Lifetime of Holiness _____
_____

What has God taught you about holiness? Are you putting His principles into practice? Is your life a reflection of His character and conduct? It is my prayer that this twelve-week Bible study has been both convicting and convincing. The Holy Spirit does the convicting of sin and sinfulness while His Word does the convincing of His power to redeem and transform. What has been your response? Are you leading a life of personal holiness?

During the writing of this study, I received a letter of confession from a friend in the ministry. He was asking for his family and his friends to forgive him for his failure. Because of personal immorality, he lost his marriage, his family, and his church. He had just realized the devastation of his sin. His pain and remorse were so apparent in his writing.

While God promises him forgiveness, my friend will experience the consequences of his sin for a long time. How can sin like that be prevented? How can other Christians avoid that mistake? We will stand up to temptation only with the help of the Holy Spirit and commitment to personal holiness. You may feel immune from immorality or separated from sinfulness. But remember your own sinful nature and the power of the evil one. Satan is prowling around looking for Christians he can devour. So be alert! Be on guard! Resist him! And keep your eyes fixed on Jesus. Determine daily to live a holy life. Only then will you be holy like God and receive His abundant blessings.

Let's discuss a few practical suggestions as you conclude this study. I would recommend that you practice these holy habits daily. While you may think of some other principles for holiness, these suggestions may help you live for Him for the rest of your life.

1. Praise and adore your Holy God regularly.
2. Understand that we are to be His holy people.
3. Accept His call for personal holiness.
4. Revere some holy heroes in the Word and the world.
5. Develop a character and conduct of holiness.
6. Pray diligently for the unholy people in this unholy world.
7. Develop daily holiness in your words and deeds.
8. Replace unholy habits with holy habits.
9. Pursue a life of holiness faithfully.
10. Enjoy the blessings of holiness.
11. Allow God to use your holiness to influence others.
12. Be holy now and for all eternity.

And remember, holiness brings far more joy than sinfulness!

Now you may ask the question: what next? What should I do now that I have completed this Bible study on holiness? The answer is simple to say but difficult to do. Persevere. Continue. Keep on. *Persevere* in your study of holiness. *Continue* to be holy in all your thoughts and actions. *Keep on* challenging others to become holy through your own words and example. If you keep on doing these things, you will be called *holy*.

This is the commitment I make to God and this is the commitment I make to you, dear friend. I commit myself to living a holy life every day from now on. Do you make that commitment? I pray that your commitment to holiness is sincere and strong. I will pray for you and will covet your prayers for me. Many blessings as you live out this holy life!

Wholly Holy

Be holy, for I am holy;
Be godly, for I am God.

Holy Father
Holy Spirit
Three in One.

Holy in being
Holy in love
Holy in life
He reigns above.

Wholly holy, He alone
Is truly holy, the Righteous One.
Because we are His
And His power is ours
We can be holy
Wholly holy
His power is ours.

FOR FURTHER THOUGHT

"Holiness is inwrought by the Holy spirit, not because we have suffered, but because we have surrendered."

—*Richard Shelley Taylor*

"How little people know who think that holiness is dull. When one meets the real thing…it is irresistible."

—*C.S. Lewis*

"If but ten among us lead a holy life, we shall kindle a fire which shall light up the entire city."

—*St. John Chrysostom*

"The greatest miracle that God can do today is to take an unholy man out of an unholy world, and make that man holy and put him back into that unholy world and keep him holy in it."

—*Leonard Ravenhill*

"It might be well if we stopped using the terms *victory* and *defeat* to describe our progress in holiness. Rather we should use the terms *obedience* and *disobedience*."

—*Jerry Bridges*

"Holiness is not freedom from temptation, but power to overcome temptation."

—*G. Campbell Morgan*

"There are no shortcuts to maturity. It takes time to be holy."

—*Erwin W. Lutzer*

"Saying yes to God means saying no to things that offend His holiness"

—*A. Morgan Derham*

"Joy not only results from a holy life, but there is also a sense in which joy helps produce a holy life."

—*Jerry Bridges*

"Holiness is the walk of faith in the life of progressive sanctification made possible in us by the Holy Spirit through obedience to the Word of God."

—*Charles F. Stanley*

"Given spiritual life, holiness means the maintaining in health of that life before God and the setting apart of that life for His service alone."

—*Stephen F. Olford*

Old Testament	New Testament	
Old Testament	**New Testament**	**OTHER SCRIPTURES ABOUT HOLINESS**
Exodus 3:5	Mark 6:20	
Exodus 15:11	Luke 4:34	
Exodus 20:8	Romans 1:2	
Leviticus 19:2	Romans 12:1–2	
Deuteronomy 7:6	2 Corinthians 7:1	
1 Samuel 2:2	Ephesians 1:4	
2 Chronicles 30:27	Colossians 3:12	
Psalm 2:6	1 Thessalonians 3:13	
Psalm 89:35	1 Thessalonians 4:7	
Psalm 93:5	1 Timothy 2:8	
Psalm 99:9	2 Timothy 1:9	
Psalm 145:21	Hebrews 12:10	
Isaiah 6:3	1 Peter 2:9	
Isaiah 30:15	Revelation 4:8	
Isaiah 35:8	Revelation 15:4	
	Revelation 21:2	
	Revelation 22:11	

This section includes some teaching suggestions for the small group leader. It also provides a format for the discussion time and a typical schedule for a one-hour session. A focus group has tried this particular approach, and it was successful. Let the Holy Spirit lead your group discussion, and make any appropriate changes. These are simply teaching helps.

LESSON ONE: A HOLY GOD

Prayer Time (5 minutes)

Ask each member of the group to write a prayer of commitment in the front of her Bible study book. Spend a few minutes in personal prayer, asking God to bless this Bible study.

Review (5 minutes)

Discuss the format for this study and details about the group meeting. Encourage each member to complete her own study before discussing it with the group.

Introduction (5 minutes)

Ask the group to call out synonyms for the word *holy*. Encourage and accept all words which reflect a scriptural or a worldly view of holiness. Write these words on an overhead or a marker board so that everyone can see them.

Group Discussion (40 minutes)

1. Discuss the literal meaning of the word *holy*. Go back to the words listed in the introduction and look up additional definitions in other dictionaries, and discuss

which ones are distortions and which definitions are accurate perceptions of holiness.

2. Read Isaiah 6:1–8 aloud. Have group members describe the holiness of God.

3. Discuss the sinless nature of God as described in Psalm 89:30–37.

4. Have group members share times when God has revealed His glory and holiness to them.

Closing (5 minutes)

1. Sing together the chorus "Our God is an Awesome God."

2. Respond to God's revelation of His holiness. Usher in a time of praise, asking group members to call out words which describe the holy character of God. Close the prayer time by reading this week's Holy Scripture for Holy Living (Is. 6:3) aloud together.

Prayer Time (5 minutes)

Give an index card to each member and ask her to record one specific prayer request. Collect the cards. Then distribute one card to each person. Pray silently for that particular need.

Review (5 minutes)

Review Lesson One by asking the following questions:

What is *holiness*?
How should we respond to the holiness of God?
Has God revealed anything new to you this week about His holiness?

Introduction (5 minutes)

Ask members to reminisce about the children's game "Follow the Leader." What were the rules of the game? What made it fun? What made it challenging? Sometimes the leader in the

LESSON TWO:
A HOLY PEOPLE

game purposely performs acts that come easily to her, but will be difficult for her followers—that is the challenge! God is our leader and we are to follow Him. Holiness seems natural for God, but impossible for us—His followers. Explain that the difference between the childhood game and following God in holiness is that instead of trying to "get us out," God actually empowers us to follow Him successfully.

Group Discussion (40 minutes)

1. Read 1 Peter 1:13–21 and ask the question: "Why are believers to be holy?"

2. Discuss the biblical teachings about God's call. Encourage members to share testimonies of God's call in their lives.

3. Discuss specific guidelines for holy conduct as given in Leviticus 19.

4. Read Matthew 26:39; 4:18–22; and John 8:11–12. Discuss the call and the commitment made in each of these passages.

Closing (5 minutes)

1. Read this week's Holy Scripture for Holy Living (1 Pet. 1:15–16) aloud together.

2. Ask each member to find a partner in the group with whom she can pray regarding their commitment to holiness. Allow time for this prayer before closing with a prayer for holy conduct among believers.

LESSON THREE: A CALL TO HOLINESS

Prayer Time (5 minutes)

Open the study with a silent time of prayer. Lead members in asking God to: confirm His holiness, convict them of their sinfulness, and call them to lives of holiness.

Review (5 minutes)

Review previous weeks' lessons by asking:

1. What thoughts have you had this week regarding God and His holiness?
2. What does the Scripture teach about holy living?

Introduction (5 minutes)

Ask the members of the class, "When you were children, what did you want to be when you grew up?" Did any ladies in the group actually fulfill those early desires? Introduce the idea of 'growing up' into holiness.

Group Discussion (40 minutes)

1. Read 1 Thessalonians 4:1–8 and discuss the Christian's call to holy living. Be sure to cover "abound more and more," (v. 1) "walk in God," (v. 1) "please God," (v. 1) and "possess your own vessel in sanctification" (v.4).

2. Read Romans 12:1–2, and discuss God's will for the believer. Contrast the phrase "be transformed" with "be conformed."

3. Ask members to answer the question: "What pleases you?" Read Philippians 4:8–9, Colossians 3:20, and Hebrews 13:21. Identify the things which please God.

4. Answer the question: "How are you living out God's call to holiness in your life?"

Closing (5 minutes)

1. Read this week's Holy Scripture for Holy Living (1 Thess. 4:7) aloud together.

2. Have a time of prayer asking God to reveal to each member ways in which she has pleased Him. Ask members to pray silently, renewing their commitment to please God through holy living.

Prayer Time (5 minutes)

Follow this model for prayer as you voice sentence prayers to the Father.

A – adoration
C – confession
T – thanksgiving
S – supplication

Review (5 minutes)

Review the previous weeks' teachings by asking:

Who is called to be holy?
Why are Christians to be holy?

Introduction (5 minutes)

Ask members, "Who is your hero? Why? Whom do you look up to because of their character and contributions?" Accept heroes from all areas of life. Then direct the discussion toward biblical heroes.

Group Discussion (40 minutes)

1. Read Luke 1:5–6. Discuss the heroic attribute of righteousness as displayed by Elizabeth. Discuss other righteous heroes and talk about what is involved in heroic righteousness.

2. Read Luke 2:36–38. Discuss the heroic attribute of service as displayed by Anna. Discuss other servant heroes and talk about what is involved in heroic servanthood.

3. Read Luke 10:38–42. Discuss the heroic attribute of commitment as displayed by Mary. Discuss other committed heroes and talk about what is involved in heroic commitment.

4. Read the quote from Corrie ten Boom. Make two columns on the board, and title them "Command" and "Provision." In the command column, write "Love your enemies." In the provision column, write "the love itself." Ask the women to name other commands God gives us, and what His provision is for keeping them.

Closing (5 minutes)

1. Read this week's Holy Scripture for Holy Living (Luke 1:6) aloud together.

2. Have a member of the group take each of the commands written on the board, and pray a sentence prayer for the other members that they would walk in that commandment, and be righteous before God, like Elizabeth.

Prayer Time (5 minutes)

Ask members to pray in "prayer triplets" (groups of three). Pray specifically for each person to be "built up in Christ."

Review (5 minutes)

Review the previous lessons by asking:

1. What are some characteristics of holy heroes?
2. Have you encountered any holy heroes this week?

Introduction (5 minutes)

Read the three-part definition of "process" given in the lesson. Have members name some processes in which they are involved (for example: redecorating a house, getting a college degree, etc.). Discuss how life itself is a series of processes.

Group Discussion (40 minutes)

1. Begin the discussion by asking, "What does it mean to be sanctified?" Develop a working definition of the word *sanctification*.

2. Read Colossians 2:20–23. Discuss the things the world turns to for sanctification.

3. Read Leviticus 20:8. Who sanctifies us?

4. Discuss the process of sanctification as described in Colossians 3:1–14.

5. Make three columns on the board with headings: Put to Death, Take Off, Put on. Have members list items in each column from the passage in Colossians 3.

6. Discuss the process of getting dressed. Point out to the class that we cannot put on a new set of clothes until we have shed the old set.

Closing (5 minutes)

1. Read this week's Holy Scripture for Holy Living (Col. 3:12) aloud together.

2. Have a time of silent prayer, asking the members to pray for the person on their left that they would take off ungodliness, then for the person on their right that they would put on godliness. Close this time of prayer by singing together "Take Time to be Holy."

LESSON SIX: AN UNHOLY WORLD

Prayer Time (5 minutes)

Spend time praying these Scriptures about holiness.

1 Peter 1:15-16; 1 Thessalonians 4:7; Luke 1:6; Colossians 3:12

Voice these Scriptures aloud and personalize them with the name of a member of the class.

Review (5 minutes)

Review the previous weeks' lessons by asking:
1. What do we know about the holiness of God?
2. What do we know about the holiness of God's people?

Introduction (5 minutes)

Distribute copies of the local newspaper, including all sections, to the members of the class. Have them skim the headlines of their sections for comments on the unholiness of the world in which we live. Point out that this is not a new phenomenon, that the world has been unholy since sin first entered the world.

Group Discussion (40 minutes)

1. Read 1 John 2:15-17. Discuss temptation, the tempter, and the result of temptation as described in Scripture.

2. Read Ephesians 6:10-17. Discuss how the believer is able to resist temptation.

3. Contrast the terms "testing" and "temptation." Stress that testing comes from God, while temptations come from Satan. Based on 1 John 2:3-11, discuss the ways a believer is tested. Stress that God can use both temptation and testing to strengthen the believer's faith.

4. Discuss the believer's triumph over testing and temptation as described in Romans 8:2; John 8:34-36; John 8:31-32; Romans 5:9; Galatians 5:13-14; and Romans 6:23.

Closing (5 minutes)

1. Read aloud together this week's Holy Scripture for Holy Living (1 John 2:15) .

2. Pray, asking God to reveal to each member of the group aspects of this world she loves. Ask Him to make each woman a holy person in an unholy world.

Prayer Time (5 minutes)

Write the following topics on index cards and give to six members of the group: Praise to God, Members of Bible study group, The church, Christian friends, Unsaved friends, Thanksgiving to God. Ask each member to voice a topical sentence prayer.

Review (5 minutes)

Review previous lessons briefly by asking these questions:
    1. Who calls us to be holy?

LESSON SEVEN:
DAILY HOLINESS

2. Who tempts us to unholiness?

3. Who gives us triumph and enables us to be holy?

Introduction (5 minutes)

Read Steve Martini's quote, "The trouble most people have resisting temptation is that they never really want to discourage it completely." Discuss the requirement of commitment in becoming holy.

Group Discussion (40 minutes)

1. Discuss the Scriptures listed in this lesson that instruct Christians as to daily conduct. What does it mean to make a daily commitment to holiness?

2. Discuss the meaning of dedication. Have members describe people they know who are truly dedicated. Make a list on the board of behaviors that members mention which indicate dedication.

3. Discuss the meaning of discipline. Discuss the difference in divine discipline and human discipline.

4. Have the members list spiritual disciplines that are necessary for daily holiness. Discuss the importance of each one.

Closing (5 minutes)

1. Read aloud together this week's Holy Scripture for Holy Living (Luke 9:23).

2. Have members form pairs, share one specific goal in a spiritual discipline, and pray together for the dedication to reach their goals.

Prayer Time (5 minutes)
Ask each person to find a prayer partner and spend time praying in this manner: Praise to God, Petition for Others, Prayer for Self.

Review (5 minutes)

Pose these questions: Has God convicted you of unholiness during this study? Have you made a genuine commitment to holy living? Would you share some specific things you've learned?

Introduction (5 minutes)

Introduce this lesson by mentioning our nation's obsession with youth. Have members list habits which we pursue energetically in order to maintain an appearance of youth. Guide members to list habits which will make us look older. Discuss the principles of holiness given from Jerry Bridges' *The Pursuit of Holiness*, but in the context of maintaining that youthful appearance. Relate this discussion to the spiritual concept of the "old man in sin and the new man in Christ." Say that we want our habits to indicate that we are new in Christ rather than old women!

Group Discussion (40 minutes)

1. Make two columns on the board with the headings: old and new. From Ephesians 4:17–32, compare and contrast the old man in sin with the new man in Christ.

2. Discuss holy habits that believers should develop through frequent repetition as suggested in this week's lesson.

3. Have members share with the group any other holy habits they would want to add to this list. How will they develop these holy habits?

Closing (5 minutes)

1. Read this week's Holy Scripture for Holy Living (Eph. 4:24) aloud together.
2. Pray, asking God to create in each member of the group a new person of true righteousness and holiness.

Prayer Time (5 minutes)

Begin this group session with a directed quiet time. Ask members to pray silently following this model written on the board:

> Praise to God
> Confession of Sin
> Requests for Self (physical needs, mental needs, spiritual needs)
> Confidence in God

Review (5 minutes)

Review the previous lesson by asking the following question. What do we need to do in order to become holy? What have been some stumbling blocks to your pursuit of personal holiness?

Introduction (5 minutes)

Ask members to list things which we actively pursue (examples: a degree, physical fitness, a bargain). Read Hebrews 12:14, and ask if we pursue holiness with the same zeal with which we pursue other goals.

Group Discussion (40 minutes)

1. Read Isaiah 6:1–8. Reflect on the posture of the seraphim as they beheld the holiness of God. In three columns on the board, prepare to describe the reverence, humility, and service demonstrated by the seraphim. At the head of your columns, write: Covered face—Reverence, Covered feet—Humility, and Flying—Service.

2. Discuss the meaning of reverence. Discuss Mary of Bethany's demonstration of reverence and the ways that we can demonstrate the same attitude of honor and respect.

3. Discuss how humility flows naturally from reverence. Discuss God's response to the humble.

4. Discuss the relationship of service to holy living. According to the Scriptures listed in this section, what is the motivation for service that is holy?

Closing (5 minutes)

1. Read this week's Holy Scripture for Holy Living (Heb. 12:14) aloud together.

2. Reflect on the multi-directional reflections of a wholehearted pursuit of holiness. Holiness reflected upward is seen in a reverence for God, holiness reflected inward is seen in a humility of self, and holiness reflected outward is seen in service to others.

Prayer Time (5 minutes)

As members come in, ask them to find Psalm 23 and spend some time meditating on this prayer of David.

Review (5 minutes)

To review previous lessons, ask members to share reasons for and results of a pursuit of holiness.

Introduction (5 minutes)

Ask members to list some examples of "the fruit of our labor" (examples may include: money, clean house, well-behaved children, a meal, etc.) This is a worldly idiom, so reflect further on "fruit" in the Bible (examples may include: the command to be fruitful and multiply, the fruit in the Garden of Eden, Fruit of the Spirit, Jesus' command to bear fruit, etc.) Challenge members to a fruity search, and offer a prize to the first person to identify Fruit Loops in this lesson (the circular nature in the production of fruit: the development of holiness produces fruit, the fruit leads to becoming more holy, which leads to more fruit, etc.). Have an elaborately wrapped box of Fruit Loops cereal to award to the winner.

LESSON TEN:
THE FRUIT OF
HOLINESS

Group Discussion (40 minutes)

1. Have individuals read aloud Philippians 1:11; James 3:18; Romans 1:13; 1 Corinthians 16:15; and John 4:36. Based on these verses, develop a group definition of *fruit*.

2. Read Galatians 5:22-23. Have members name ways that each aspect of the Fruit of the Spirit is manifested in their lives.

3. Focus on joy, and discuss the difference between joy and happiness. Discuss sources of joy and talk about what robs us of joy (John 15:10–11 and Ps. 51:8,12).

4. Discuss the meaning of wisdom. Read James 3:13–18 and discuss the difference between heavenly wisdom and earthly wisdom.

5. Discuss the relationship of freedom and holiness according to Romans 6:22.

6. Discuss how the fruit of holiness will be seen in a believer's worship, walk, and work.

Closing (5 minutes)

1. Read this week's Holy Scripture for Holy Living (Rom. 6:22) aloud together.

2. If no one has identified Fruit Loops, explain the concept of the circular nature in the production of fruit.

LESSON ELEVEN: THE INFLUENCE OF HOLINESS

Prayer Time (5 minutes)

For today's prayer time, slowly and prayerfully repeat aloud together "The Lord's Prayer" (Matt. 6:9-13).

Review (5 minutes)

Review previous lessons by asking the following question. "How do we experience joy in personal holiness, when the world sometimes views it as boring or strange?

Introduction (5 minutes)

Ask women to list things which influenced how they dressed today (ex: the weather, lunch plans, what was clean, etc.). Ask them to name people who have had a profound influence on their lives (encourage both negative and positive examples).

Group Discussion (40 minutes)

1. Discuss the relationship between *power* and *influence*.

2. From the Scripture given in the lesson, how does our personal holiness empower us to witness?

3. Have someone read aloud Matthew 25:31–46. Discuss how God will judge His people. On the board, make two columns. In the first, list the specific needs identified in this passage. In the second, list specific ways your group is serving or can begin serving the needy.

4. Discuss the power of Jesus' love for the Samaritan woman as described in John 4:27–30. Ask members to contemplate how they have experienced the power of His love in their own lives.

5. Read 1 John 4:7–21. Ask members to identify why and how believers are to love one another. Ask if they are ever afraid to love others. Offer verses 17 and 18 as the supernatural answer to this natural fear. Emphasize that loving our brother (or sister) is a command (v. 21) and that God empowers us to keep His commands.

6. Take some time to share brief testimonies.

7. Discuss challenges of sharing our faith and being a witness.

Closing (5 minutes)

1. Read aloud together this week's Holy Scripture for Holy Living (Ps. 111:9).

2. Pray that your group's witness, service, and love will reflect God's holiness to the world.

Prayer Time (5 minutes)

Today's opening prayer will be for unbelievers. Suggest that each person write down the name of one unsaved friend then spend some time praying for their salvation. Ask God to help your holy life be a witness to her.

Review (5 minutes)

Review previous lessons by asking questions about holiness. (i.e.: *Who* is holy? *What* is holiness? *Where* are we holy? *When* did we become holy? *Why* are we holy? etc.)

Introduction (5 minutes)

Continue asking "wh–" questions. Ask, *when* did God become holy? *When* will He stop being holy? Illustrate the importance of longevity by asking your group about the length of things like movies, diets, marriages, books, time at college, sermons, and so forth. Mention that we often judge the value of things by their length. Some things are better if they are longer, while others are better if they are shorter. Point out that it is not the length of time, but its length of influence that matters. We can further understand holiness as we look at its longevity. God has always been holy. God will always be holy.

Group Discussion (40 minutes)

1. Have one part of the group look up and read Isaiah's proclamation of God's holiness in Isaiah 6:1-8 and another part of the group look up and read Revelation 4:1-11. Identify phrases which refer to the longevity of God's holiness.

2. Read 1 John 2:15-17 aloud. Ask members to point out what will pass away and what will last forever. Discuss how this is a key to holiness that will last a lifetime.

3. Discuss the heritage which Timothy received from Lois and Eunice. Ask members to share from their own heritage. Because it is likely that there will be women in your group who do not have a family heritage of holiness, ask

also for members to share about someone in their background who "passed the faith" along to them.

4. Review the doctrinal truths of justification, sanctification, and glorification. Ask members to share the truths about glorification seen in 1 Corinthians 15:50–58.

5. Read 1 Corinthians 15:58 aloud. Discuss the things that cause us to move from the path of holiness and make us tire in the work of the Lord. Read the verse again in another version as an encouragement that our "labor is not in vain."

Closing (5 minutes)

1. Ask members to share what they have learned about holiness in this study.

2. Ask for practical suggestions they have or intend to incorporate in order to become holy.

3. Close with a prayer for members to continue in their study and pursuit of holiness. Close your prayer by reading or saying this week's Holy Scripture for Holy Living (Rev. 4:8) aloud together.

This section will provide specific answers to direct questions in each lesson. The responses were compiled from Scripture and other biblical sources. Some of the questions solicit personal perspective, so there is no one correct answer. These answers are not included. A key is provided to give you additional insights into personal holiness.

**LESSON ONE:
A HOLY GOD**

Based on Psalm 89:30–37, describe the sinless character of God (fill in blanks):
    lovingkindness, faithfulness, covenant, word, holiness, lie.

**LESSON FIVE:
DEVELOPING
HOLINESS**

From Colossians 3:5, list some of the sins which should no longer be a part of the believer's life:
    immorality, impurity, passion, evil desire, greed.

From Colossians 3:8–9, list the acts of ungodliness Paul says to take off (personal examples not included here):
    anger, wrath, malice, slander, abusive speech, lying.

**LESSON SEVEN:
DAILY HOLINESS**

Daily lessons from Scripture:
    Psalm 61:8 - *fulfill commitment*
    Psalm 72:15 - *pray daily, and praise spiritual leaders*
    Psalm 88: 8–9 - *call upon the Lord every day*
    Isaiah 58:2 - *seek God daily, know His will daily, delight in Him daily*
    Mark 14:49 - *be in His presence every day - teach His Word daily*
    Luke 9:23 - *come after Him, deny self, take up His cross - follow Him daily*

Acts 2:46–47 - *bring people into the church daily*
Acts 17:11 - *study the Bible daily, make daily application*
Hebrews 3:12–13 - *exhort one another daily*
Hebrews 10:11 - *daily sacrifice, ministering daily*

Holy habits from Scripture (fill in the blank):

1. *truth*
2. *truth, lie*
3. *loving*
4. *wholesome*
5. *thoughts*
6. *immoral*
7. *encourage*
8. *positive*
9. *strong*
10. *careful*
11. *diligently*
12. *quiet*
13. *memorize*
14. *obey*
15. *worship*
16. *fellowship*
17. *always*
18. *neighbor*
19. *testimony*
20. *loving*
21. *others, you*
22. *generous*
23. *discipline*
24. *forgive, forgives*
25. *joyful, joy*

How God rewards the humble (fill in the blank):
exalts, lift, due

Heavenly wisdom is: *pure, peaceable, gentle, unwavering, reasonable*

Earthly wisdom is: *selfish, distorted, boastful, jealous*

BIBLIOGRAPHY

Abraham, Ken. *Positive Holiness*. Old Tappan, NJ: Fleming H. Revell, 1988.

Allen, Catherine B. *The New Lottie Moon*. Nashville, TN: Broadman Press, 1980.

Baxter, J. Sidlow. *A New Call to Holiness*. Grand Rapids, MI: Zondervan Publishing House, 1967.

Brengle, Samuel Logan. *Heart Talks on Holiness*. London: Salvationist Publishing and Supplies, 1897.

Bridges, Jerry. *The Pursuit of Holiness*. Colorado Springs, Co: NavPress, 1978.

Bridges, Jerry. *The Pursuit of Holiness – Study Guide*. Colorado Springs, Co: NavPress, 1978.

Drury, Keith. *Holiness for Ordinary People*. Grand Rapids, MI: Francis Asbury, Press, 1983.

Dunning, H. Ray. *Grace, Faith, and Holiness*. Kansas City, MO: Beacon Hill Press of Kansas City, 1988.

Fenhagen, James C. *Invitation to Holiness*. San Francisco: Harper and Row Publishers, 1985.

Hauerwas, Stanley. *Sanctify Them in the Truth: Holiness Exemplified*. Nashville, TN: Abingdon Press, 1998.

Holman Bible Dictionary. Nashville, TN: Holman Bible Publishers, 1991.

Ironside, H.A. *Holiness: The False and the True*. New York: Loizeaux Brothers, Inc., 1953.

Kelley, Rhonda H. *Divine Discipline: How to Develop and Maintain Self–Control*. Gretna, LA: Pelican Publishing Company, 1992.

Kelley, Rhonda H. *Life Lessons from Women in the Bible*. Nashville, TN: LifeWay Press, 1998.

Kelley, Rhonda H. *A Woman's Guide to Spiritual Wellness: A Personal Study of Colossians*. Birmingham, AL: New Hope Press, 1998.

Koeberle, Adolf. *The Quest for Holiness*. St. Louis, MO: Concordia Press, 1982.

Larsen, Earnest. *Holiness*. New York: Paulist Press, 1975.

McClung, Floyd. *Holiness and the Spirit of the Age.* Eugene, OR: Harvest House Publishers, 1990.

Merriam–Webster's Collegiate Dictionary. Springfield, MA: Merriam–Webster, 1997.

Moore, Beth. *Living Beyond Yourself: Exploring the Fruit of the Spirit.* Nashville, TN: Lifeway Press, 1998.

Morgan, Hugh D. *The Holiness of God and His People.* Wales: Evangelical Press of Wales, 1979.

Morgan, John. *Holiness Acceptable to God.* Minneapolis, MN: Bethany House Publishers, 1986.

Murray, Andrew. *The Believer's Secret of Holiness.* Minneapolis, MN: Bethany House Publishers, 1984.

Neill, Stephen. *Christian Holiness.* London: Lutterworth Press, 1960.

Olford, Stephen F. *The Way of Holiness.* Wheaton, IL: Crossway Books, 1998.

Packer, J.I. *Knowing God.* Downers Grove, IL: InterVarsity Press, 1993.

Parsons, Martin. *The Call to Holiness.* Grand Rapids, MI: William B. Eerdmans Publishing Company, 1974.

Prior, Kenneth. *The Way of Holiness.* Downers Grove, IL: InterVarsity Press, 1973.

Reed, Gerard. *C.S. Lewis and the Bright Shadow of Holiness.* Kansas City, MO: Beacon Hill Press of Kansas City, 1999.

Roseveare, Helen. *Living Holiness.* Minneapolis, MN: Bethany House Publishers, 1986.

Ryle, J.C. *Holiness.* London: James Clarke & Co., 1952.

Sproul, R.C. *The Holiness of God.* Wheaton, IL: Tyndale House Publishers, 1985.

Sproul, R.C. *Pleasing God.* Wheaton, IL: Tyndale House Publishers, 1988.

Tada, Joni Eareckson. *Holiness in Hidden Places.* Dallas, TX: Word Books, 1999.

Ten Boom, Corrie. *The Hiding Place.* Washington Depot, CT: Chosen Books, 1971.

Tracy, Wesley D. et al. *The Upward Call: Spiritual Formation and the Holy Life.* Kansas City, MO: Beacon Hill of Kansas City, 1994.

Trevethan, Thomas L. *The Beauty of God's Holiness.* Downers Grove, IL: InterVarsity Press, 1995.

White, John. *The Pathway of Holiness: A Guide for Sinners.* Downers Grove, IL: InterVarsity Press, 1996.

Wilkinson, Bruce. *Personal Holiness in Times of Temptation.* Eugene, OR: Harvest House, 1998.

The Woman's Study Bible. Nashville, TN: Thomas Nelson Publishers, 1995.

Zodhiates, Spiros. *The Hebrew–Greek Key Study Bible.* Chattanooga, TN: AMG Publishers, 1984.

NOTES